102
READING
RESPONSE
LESSONS

102
READING
RESPONSE
LESSONS

Improving
Comprehension
Skills for
Test Day—
and Beyond

KRISTIN NOELLE WOLFGANG

CORWIN PRESS
A SAGE Publications Company
Thousand Oaks, California

For information:

Corwin Press
A Sage Publications Company
2455 Teller Road
Thousand Oaks, California 91320
www.corwinpress.com

Sage Publications Ltd.
1 Oliver's Yard
55 City Road
London EC1Y 1SP
United Kingdom

Sage Publications India Pvt. Ltd.
B-42, Panchsheel Enclave
Post Box 4109
New Delhi 110 017 India

Printed in the United States of America

Library of Congress Cataloging-in-Publication Data

Wolfgang, Kristin Noelle
102 reading response lessons: Improving comprehension skills for test day—and beyond / Kristin Noelle Wolfgang.
    p. cm.
Includes bibliographical references and index.
ISBN 1-4129-2550-9 (cloth)—ISBN 1-4129-2551-7 (pbk.)
    1. Reading comprehension—Study and teaching (Elementary) 2. Reading comprehension—Ability testing. I. Title: One hundred two reading response lessons. II. Title.
LB1573.7.W65 2006
372.47—dc22

                                                    2005019384

This book is printed on acid-free paper.

05   06   07   08   09   10   9   8   7   6   5   4   3   2   1

Acquisitions Editor:	Kylee Liegl
Editorial Assistant:	Jamie Cuvier
Production Editor:	Laureen Shea
Copy Editor:	Brenda Weight
Typesetter:	C&M Digitals (P) Ltd.
Proofreader:	Kristin Bergstad
Cover Designer:	Michael Dubowe

Contents

---

*Reading response lessons marked by an asterisk have anchor pieces in Chapter 7.

Preface

102 Reading Response Lessons: Improving Comprehension Skills for Test Day—and Beyond empowers students to analyze any comprehension question and respond in clear, supported paragraphs. Teachers of Grades 3 through 12 will find the resources useful.

As a fifth-grade teacher, I find that my students struggle to comprehend what they read and to translate their comprehension into written words. The Hawai'i[1] Department of Education issues a list of 129 sample constructed-response questions that my students are expected to respond to in writing. I have seen similar lists for many other states. Countless teachers throw up their hands in frustration. If your students don't understand what to do when faced with a reading response question and you don't know what to try next to help them, this book is for you.

In 30-minute sessions, students practice test taking while learning critical and higher-order thinking skills. Students progress through the levels of Bloom's Taxonomy as the difficulty of the questions increases. Questions are provided for all three types of genres: narrative, informational, and functional. Scaffolding is provided to build skills to the independence level required by standardized testing. The scaffolding includes necessary vocabulary instruction to guide students through one of the hardest parts of reading response: understanding the questions! After students write their responses, they use a rubric, the same rubric each time, to assess their own work. Included in the rubric are the six traits of writing developed by Vicky Spandel to help students recognize what good writing is. Students can record their scores and practice the specific skills they are lacking. This

---

1. In the Hawaiian language, the 'okina (apostrophe) is considered a consonant and denotes a glottal stop between letters, hence Hawai'i is the correct spelling.

process of self-assessment and goal setting moves students through the levels of Bloom's Taxonomy and the provided scaffolding toward evaluation and independence.

I invite you to flip back to the response sheets beginning in Chapter 9 to get a clear understanding of how the questions are deconstructed. You may also want to look at Chapter 7, which includes anchors for 34 of the questions to help you and your students recognize "good" answers.

Try a few of the response sheets with your class, using the suggested titles from Chapter 6. You will see immediate improvement in how well students can respond when they understand the questions and expectations.

Acknowledgments

I am eternally grateful to all my students, who have been a tremendous help in trying out new ideas and who are always willing participants in reading response. They have been my inspiration, cheerleaders, and insightful teachers. The fifth graders of Ka'u High and Pahala Elementary from school years 2003–2004 and 2004–2005 have been integral participants in "the book."

I'd especially like to thank students who provided the anchor pieces found in Chapter 7: Layla Abellera, Berehan Anteneh, Dillin Ballo, Jenny Castaneda, Meghann Chow, Moses Espaniola, Joyce Ibasan, Pilialoha Kailiawa, Le'sha Naboa, Nicole Stein, Mahealani Taganas, Kane Thomas, and Robyn Zumwalt.

All the teachers and staff at our small school in the country have always been completely supportive and helpful. I couldn't have done it without the encouragement of Jane McKinney, Cheryl Maesaka, Darlene Javar, Calvin Keet, Roslyn Moresh, Roxanne Kala, Brenna, Gorreson, Mary Ibarra, Sandra Tamondong, JoAnn Clemens, Gloria Camba, Ruth DeMattos, Frances Volpe, Renwick Bibilone, Ted Bennett, and Jessica Smith. I also appreciate the support of our stellar administrators, Josephine DeMorales and Jim Bertilacci.

My sister Lori Kantor lent her exceptional editing skills when this book was only a proposal. I guess writing does run in the family.

My mom and dad, Joyce and Robert, were my first teachers and are still teaching me today. Thanks. Without your example, I wouldn't be me.

My editor, Kylee Liegl, and her assistant, Jaime Cuvier, threw me a rope when I needed it and pulled me through the tough book-writing process.

My writing group, the Sundae Writers, Darlene Javar, Jacquolyn McMurray, and Lora Bristow, who volunteer to read everything I write, tell me honestly what they think and host fabulous writing retreats. I can't think what I would do without them.

And, finally, a super-special thank you to my husband, Kea, and our son, Kea, who always understood when I had to work on the "the book" for just another hour and couldn't wash the dishes or watch a movie. It's been a very busy year and I'm looking forward to relaxing with you both now.

To everyone: mahalo for your support, help, advice, patience, aloha, and love!

Corwin Press gratefully acknowledges the contributions of the following reviewers:

Elizabeth Liberti
Secondary Reading
  Specialist
Williamson County
  Schools
Franklin, TN

Sue Reed
English Teacher
Trenton High School
Trenton, FL

Gordon Dasher
Classroom Teacher
Trenton High School
Trenton, FL

Elise Wajid
Regional Coordinator
Reading First
New Jersey Department
  of Education
Sewell, NJ

Denise Beasley
English, Journalism, Writing
  Teacher
Osseo Fairchild High School
Osseo, WI

Kim C. Romero, NBCT
English Teacher
Jack Britt High School
Cumberland County, NC

About the Author

 **Kristin Noelle Wolfgang** is currently the fifth-grade teacher at Ka'u High and Pahala Elementary in Pahala, Hawai'i and is a member of her school's inservice training team. She serves as the Grade Level Chair. She has also been a Cooperating Teacher for preservice teachers.

Kristin is a member of the Hawai'i Island Writer's Association (HIWA), the Hawai'i Island and International Reading Association (IRA), and Bamboo Ridge.

She's a founding member of the Sundae Writers, who meet monthly to critique their writing together. She writes short fiction, children's fiction, poetry, and essays, and intends to be published in those areas as well as in teaching resources.

Her backpacking adventures have taken her from the Appalachian Trail to Volcanoes National Park.

This is her first book.

SECTION 1

Guiding Reading Response in Your Classroom

An Introduction 1

"I want to teach my students to do
well on the test, but I'm against the idea of 'teaching to the test.'"

"I can keep them reading,
but they can't answer those test questions!"

"How do I get from a list of questions to helping
my students truly understand how to answer those questions?"

"My students don't even understand
the vocabulary in the questions!"

Have you had these thoughts? Maybe you've had these conversations
with your colleagues, with your friends, or even with your administrators?
Read on and discover a process that will give your students the skills to
take apart any reading response question and answer in organized, clear
paragraphs. Your students will be prepared to answer comprehension
questions both in daily classwork and on standardized tests!

Overview

Organized Into 30-Minute Lessons

10 minutes: Teacher introduces the response sheet and leads class discussion

10 minutes: Teacher reads selected text aloud or students read silently

10 minutes: Students respond to the question

Includes 102 Questions

Teacher chooses question order, format, and schedule

Provides Built-In Scaffolding

Starts with teacher reading aloud

Progresses to teacher reading aloud while students read along silently

Accelerates to students reading independently

Prepares Students for Statewide Assessment

Supports Standards-Based Learning

Builds Reading and Writing Skills Simultaneously

Meets Needs for Teacher Flexibility

- Useful across content areas in any class
- Language arts, reading
- GT, ESLL, special education
- **Wherever you need it!**

Development

Faced with the tremendous task of helping fifth graders broaden their reading response capabilities, I developed a process that teaches students to analyze any constructed response question and synthesize their answers into clear, well-supported paragraphs. *102 Reading Response Lessons* applies this process by dismantling 102 questions into ready-made, easy-to-teach lessons.

This reading response process consists of five steps that take 30 minutes:

1. Students review the vocabulary words on the response sheets with their teacher. Each response sheet addresses one constructed response question, so the students gain an understanding of each word and begin to plan how to respond.

2. The class reviews the Reading Response Rubric together so expectations are clear about what should be included in the students' responses.

3. The teacher reads an appropriate book aloud. The students progress to reading texts independently. The 102 lessons include questions that address all three genres: narrative, informational, and functional. Chapter 6 includes suggested texts for each question type.

4. Each student writes his or her response with the support of the response sheet and the rubric.

5. The teacher guides the students in self-assessment using the rubric. Chapter 7 contains examples of quality work.

After applying this process of written response, my students' response writing skills improved considerably, as evidenced by their rubric scores. The rubric provides an authentic assessment tool for teachers to document their students' progress.

My students have become accustomed to breaking down each question for understanding, responding in a clearly written paragraph, and assessing their own work. These are higher-order thinking skills that today's students need to succeed.

The data collection charts in Chapter 5 facilitate the management of assessment data.

Development of the Process

I created *102 Reading Response Lessons* while working with my fifth-grade students. I started by reading picture books aloud and analyzing a few reading response questions on the board. The students listed synonyms for the words in the question. We then discussed what the question meant and what a good answer would include.

The first constructed response question I chose was "Explain how the author's message connects to your own life" because *author's message* is mentioned specifically in the state standards of Hawai'i, where

I teach. After reading my students' responses, I realized that we would need to repeat the exercise several times before they could really grasp the meaning of *author's message*. We repeated the question a total of five times before my students were writing quality responses.

I found that using picture books with explicit authors' messages supported my students' understanding. *The Berenstain Bears and Too Much TV* by Stan and Jan Berenstain has an explicit author's message. After using passages with very clear authors' messages, the students were able to succeed with passages in which the author's message was more difficult to infer.

In developing our rubric, my students and I determined that a quality response would show an understanding of the question, begin with a thesis statement, and include at least three supporting details from the book. Although I believe that what students have to say is far more important than their punctuation, spelling, and grammar, we included conventions criteria because responses have to be readable.

As I shared this process with my colleagues, they encouraged me to publish the process so other teachers and students could benefit from it as well.

Planning and Implementation 2

Phase One

Read the text to the class. Reading aloud will provide scaffolding for the readers with special needs and auditory learners in your class.

Phase Two

Repeat the process, selecting progressively more difficult questions. Use included anchor pieces (on the overhead projector or copied) to show your students a good response. Have students work independently or with partners. It is important for students to practice finding examples from the texts to support their theses. Repeat a question if your students had trouble responding. (Skip questions that you are sure your students have learned in other areas of your class.) There are great benefits in repeated questions, and students love the challenge of making their scores higher each time.

Phase Three

Use the response sheets with blank vocabulary boxes. Students can generate their own synonyms for the vocabulary, giving you a way to check their prior knowledge and understanding. Once your students can respond to the questions without the response sheets, build toward independence and generalization by assigning a list of questions, found in Chapter 8, as independent work.

Suggested Texts

In Chapter 6, you will find a list of texts, including picture books. Regardless of grade level, picture books help students learn because they are fast and clear examples.

Response Sheets

The response sheet, shown in Figure 2.1, is a powerful graphic organizer. There are two response sheets for each of the 102 reading response questions in this book.

Figure 2.1   Response Sheet

Name _____   **Analysis: Narrative**

Explain how the author's message connects to your own life.

Vocabulary Box

explain	decide how, judge, tell, describe
author's message	what the author wanted you to learn, the moral of the story
connects to your own life	relates to your life, makes sense in your own life, could be useful for your own life

Student-Friendly Translation

Decide and describe how the moral of the story could be useful in your own life. Give details from the story and from your life to explain.

This means:

Think about the moral of the story. What is the story about and what did you learn from it? How does that message connect to your life? What lesson from the story could you use in your life? Remember, it is okay to make something up if you need to! Give details from the story to support your ideas.

Write, write, write, explain, explain, explain!

In Phase One, use the vocabulary box, shown in Figure 2.2. Students are given familiar synonyms. This helps students see relationships between words used. For instance, the first word in most response questions asks students to think about the text—decide, judge, describe, and so on.

Figure 2.2   Vocabulary Box

Explain how the author's message connects to your own life.

Vocabulary Box

explain	decide how, judge, tell, describe
author's message	what the author wanted you to learn, the moral of the story
connects to your own life	relates to your life, makes sense in your own life, could be useful for your own life

The student-friendly translation box, in Figure 2.3, presents the complete question using the synonyms from the vocabulary box.

Figure 2.3   Student-Friendly Translation

Student-Friendly Translation

> Decide and describe how the moral of the story could be useful in your own life. Give details from the story and from your life to explain.

The "this means" box, shown in Figure 2.4, gives ideas that help students understand what is expected of them.

Figure 2.4   "This Means" Box

This means:

> Think about the moral of the story. What is the story about and what did you learn from it? How does that message connect to your life? What lesson from the story could you use in your life? Remember, it is okay to make something up if you need to! Give details from the story to support your ideas.

Each page ends with the encouragement to "Write, write, write, explain, explain, explain" as shown in Figure 2.1 because so many of our students sell themselves short by not giving enough information.

In Phase Three, use the second response sheet, which has a blank vocabulary box (shown in Figure 2.5) for each question. Check your students' prior knowledge before you discuss it in class.

Figure 2.5   Vocabulary Box, Phase Three

Vocabulary Box

explain	
author's message	
connects to your own life	

Anchor Pieces

When a student achieves a score of 3 or 4 on the rubric, post his or her response in your classroom with a rubric and your comments so that other students can see what a good answer looks like. In Phases One and Two, these anchor pieces are very important so that students can see complete responses written by other students. Copy these anchor pieces onto transparencies to use for instruction, pointing out the thesis statements and details from the text. Create an anchor piece collection of your own.

I have included my collection of anchor pieces in Chapter 7 for you to use with your students. These are student-written anchor pieces for selected questions so teachers and students can clearly recognize quality work. The first four anchors show the anchors in plain text as well as marked with underlining and italics. The thesis statement is underlined and the supporting details are set in italics to give you an idea of how to mark the anchors for your students. The remainder of the anchors are in plain text; you can mark these in handouts or on the overhead or use them plain. Use the anchor pieces from Chapter 7 or your own collection to reteach before repeating questions in Phase Two.

Rubrics

The Reading Response Rubric, shown in Figure 2.6, is used for assessing every written response. In Chapter 4, I have included three variations of this rubric because I know every teacher has his or her own particular style. This rubric was designed to assess what is important in written response: a thesis statement (or topic sentence), the amount and quality of examples (or details) that support the thesis, clear understanding of the question, and the use of writing techniques to enhance the student's writing.

Figure 2.6   Reading Response Rubric

Reading Response Rubric

Score _____   Name _____

4 = Exceeds	• Meets all indicators for a score of 3.
	• Gives more than three details from the story.
	• Uses *some* of the six traits of writing to enhance his or her writing, such as the following:
	  • Ideas—the essay contains sensory details.
	  • Organization—there is an interesting lead and conclusion.
	  • Voice—the essay sounds like this unique writer.
	  • Word choice—vocabulary used by this writer is engaging.
	  • Sentence fluency—the essay is smooth, and the sentences are different lengths.
	  • Conventions—spelling, punctuation, and so forth are excellent.

3 = Meets	• Contains a thesis statement (topic sentence). • Shows clear understanding of the question and can respond to it. • Gives three details from the story to support the thesis statement. • Conventions make the piece readable.
2 = Approaching	• There is no thesis statement (topic sentence). • It is not clear that the writer understood the question. • Gives 0–2 details from the story that would support a thesis statement.
1 = Needs Work	• The writer didn't understand the question. • There are no details that support the thesis.
Teacher's Commentary	

Using Six Traits

A response that exceeds these expectations earns a score of 4. It includes writing that is enhanced with use of the six traits of writing developed by Vicky Spandel (ideas, organization, voice, word choice, sentence fluency, and conventions).

When one of my students responded to *When I Was Young in the Mountains* by Cynthia Rylant with a story about a time he spent with his grandparents up in the mountain and killed a wild boar to bring home for dinner, his response included so much voice, it was as if he were sitting at lunch telling us the story. This response is included in Chapter 7.

Other times, students describe things so well with sensory details that the response transcends the academic genre and becomes a narrative.

You may have students who choose specific and excellent vocabulary (word choice), use a variety of sentence lengths (sentence fluency), or have excellent conventions.

I don't usually score for organization because the rubric already demands well-organized essays. But if a student includes excellent transitions and a conclusion, organization could move a score 3 paper to a score 4.

Data Collection

I have designed a simple data collection system that reports your data in three ways.

- The Data Collection Chart, shown in Figure 2.7, shows the question, text, and each student's score. This is similar to a grade book.

N is Needs Work, A is Approaching, M is Meets, and E is Exceeds.

- The Class Summary Data Chart, Figure 2.8, is a way of showing the class how they are doing as a group without showing individual scores. Students enjoy watching the class scores in Exceeds increase as the scores in Needs Work disappear. They also notice when the scores drop after an especially difficult question.

- The students record their own score on the Individual Data Chart, shown in Figure 2.9, in their language arts portfolio.

Figure 2.7   Data Collection Chart

Book Title	Too Much TV, Berenstains	Fine School, Creech				
Question	Author's Message	How Did Your Opinion Change?				
Meghann	A	M				
Joyce	M	M				
Layla	M	E				
Mahea	N	N				
Pili	N	A				
Berehan	M	A				
Kea	E	E				

Figure 2.8 Class Summary Data Chart

Book Title	Too Much TV	Fine School												
Question Number	1	1												
Exceeds	1	2												
Meets	3	2												
Approaching	1	2												
Needs Work	2	1												

Figure 2.9   Individual Data Chart

Title and Date	Too Much TV 12/1	Fine School 1/5										
4												
3												
2												
1												

Independent Reading Logs

After years of struggling with reading logs, I found a method that works for me and includes the reading response process. As a part of Phase Three, every night my students read for at least 30 minutes. Then they write a response to a question glued into their reading logs. I require that they write 14 lines. They must complete each of the assigned questions at least once each quarter. I check their log every morning and record the number of the question that they answered. My students gain extra practice in the reading response process by answering questions about their independent reading. You will find a list of questions ready to use in Chapter 8.

Teacher Flexibility

You don't have to use all the response sheets or even collect data using the charts. My goal was to design a system that other teachers can use in their own classrooms in whatever way works best for them. For instance, if you don't like the rubric, fashion one that works for you.

There are 102 questions in this book, and most of us have about 135 days from the beginning of the year until April 1, when statewide testing traditionally begins.

I purposefully built teacher input and flexibility into this curriculum because every teacher, class, and school is different. Some reading curricula include response, and students in those classes are very familiar with the questions and how to answer. Other curricula may touch on some critical response questions, but not in writing. Many teachers use oral response or discussion, but testing is based on written response, so the practice of this process is crucial.

My students and I have made a great leap into written reading response. They continue to surprise me with their insightful writing. Give your students the chance to surprise you also by remembering that no matter what your situation, whether you work with high achievers or English language learners, children can learn to respond to texts if they are provided with scaffolding, remarkable books to spark their interests, and opportunities to practice.

Lesson Plans 3

Reading Response Lesson Plan: Phase One

Materials Needed:

Response sheets: one per student (see Chapters 9–23)

Rubric: one per student (see Chapter 4)

Text for reading (see Chapter 6 for suggested titles)

Introduction: Pass out the response sheets and the rubrics (10 minutes)

1. Read the response question to the class.

2. Vocabulary box: Review synonyms for the vocabulary in the box.

3. Student-friendly translation: Restate the response question.

4. This means: Give "teacher talk ideas" to help students understand the question and its nuances.

5. Go over score points 3 and 4 on the rubric with the students so they know your expectations. Be sure that they know what a thesis statement (or topic sentence) is and how to find examples in the passage.

6. Introduce the text that you are using today.

Read (10 minutes)

7. Read the text aloud.

Respond (10–15 minutes)

8. Ask the students to respond in writing; emphasize the need for details from the passage.

Closure

9. Ask students to underline their thesis statement and put stars next to their examples. Have students share their theses.

10. Have students self-assess, using the rubric. Ask them to circle the indicators they feel they have achieved.

Assessment

11. Read the students' self-assessments; if you agree, star the indicators that they circled and write their score on the top.

Reading Response Lesson Plan: Phase Two

Using Anchor Pieces

Materials Needed:

Response sheets: one per student (see Chapters 9–23)

Rubric: one per student (see Chapter 4)

Text for reading (see Chapter 6 for suggested titles)

Anchor piece transparency (see Chapter 7)

Introduction: Pass out the response sheets and the rubrics (10 minutes)

1. Follow the introduction steps in the Phase One lesson plan.

2. Put the anchor piece transparency on the overhead projector.

3. Read the anchor piece aloud to the students.

4. Ask the students to point out the thesis statement and the three details used by the writer.

Read (10 minutes)

5. Read the text aloud or have students read independently.

Respond (10–15 minutes)

   6. Ask the students to respond in writing; emphasize the need for details from the passage and a thesis statement.

Closure

   7. Ask students to underline their thesis statement and put stars next to their examples. Have students share their theses.

   8. Have students self-assess, using the rubric. Ask them to circle the indicators they feel they have achieved.

Assessment

   9. Read the students' self-assessments; if you agree, star the indicators that they circled and write their score on the top.

Reading Response Lesson Plan: Phase Three

Materials Needed:

   Response sheets: one per student (see Chapters 9–23)

   Rubric: one per student (see Chapter 4)

   Text for reading (see Chapter 6 for suggested titles)

Introduction: Pass out the response sheets and the rubrics (10 minutes)

   1. Read the response question to the class.

   2. Vocabulary box: Have students produce familiar synonyms for the vocabulary in the box.

   3. Student-friendly translation: Restate the response question.

   4. This means: Give "teacher talk ideas" to help students understand the question and its nuances.

   5. Go over score points 3 and 4 on the rubric with the students so they know your expectations. Be sure that they know what a thesis statement (or topic sentence) is and how to find examples in the passage.

   6. Introduce the text that you are using today.

Read (10 minutes)

    7. Read the text aloud or have students read independently.

Respond (10–15 minutes)

    8. Ask the students to respond in writing; emphasize the need for details from the passage and a thesis statement.

Closure

    9. Ask students to underline their thesis statement and put stars next to their examples. Have students share their theses.

  10. Have students self-assess, using the rubric. Ask them to circle the indicators they feel they have achieved.

Assessment

  11. Read the students' self-assessments; if you agree, star the indicators that they circled and write their score on the top.

One Rubric for Every Response 4

The following rubrics were designed specifically for the reading response process. My students and I selected the qualities that we considered important in the response pieces. But I also examined rubrics used for reading response on statewide assessments for various states. The most important elements are details from the text that support the student's thesis. This is also the difficult part for most students.

The first and most comprehensive rubric includes all the indicators for each score point.

The second, half-page rubric employs the grid style preferred by some teachers.

The third rubric is in a checklist format with two variations of what students need to include to meet the goal. Students do better when we tell them what we expect. The first variation uses the words *thesis statement,* and the second variation uses the words *topic sentence.* Use the variation that best matches your state standards.

Choose the rubric that works best for you or feel free to make a rubric of your own. You, as the teacher, know your expectations best. What is important is that you communicate them to your students.

Reading Response Rubric

Score _____   Name _____

4 = Exceeds	• Meets all indicators for a score of 3.
	• Gives more than three details from the story.
	• Uses *some* of the six traits of writing to enhance his or her writing, such as the following:
	  • Ideas—the essay contains sensory details.
	  • Organization—there is an interesting lead and conclusion.
	  • Voice—the essay sounds like this unique writer.
	  • Word choice—vocabulary used by this writer is engaging.
	  • Sentence fluency—the essay is smooth, and the sentences are different lengths.
	  • Conventions—spelling, punctuation, and so forth are excellent.

3 = Meets	• Contains a thesis statement (topic sentence). • Shows clear understanding of the question and can respond to it. • Gives three details from the story to support the thesis statement. • Conventions make the piece readable.
2 = Approaching	• There is no thesis statement (topic sentence). • It is not clear that the writer understood the question. • Gives 0–2 details from the story that would support a thesis statement.
1 = Needs Work	• The writer didn't understand the question. • There are no details that support the thesis.
Teacher's Commentary	

Name _____   Score _____

Reading Response	Needs Work	Approaching	Meets	Exceeds
Thesis statement (topic sentence)	No thesis statement	No thesis statement	Contains thesis statement	Clear thesis statement
Understanding of the question and how to respond to it	Writer doesn't understand the question	It is not clear that the writer understood the question	Writer shows a clear understanding of the question and can respond to it	Writer shows a clear understanding of the question and responds to it effectively
Details from text	There are no details that support the thesis	There are 0–2 details from the text that support the thesis	There are three details from the story that support the thesis	There are more than three details that support the thesis statement
Use of writing techniques (six traits)				The writer uses one or more of the six traits to enhance the writing piece

Reading Response Checklist

☐ I started with a thesis statement.

☐ I understand what the question means.

☐ I included three details from the story that support my thesis statement.

☐ My conventions make the piece readable.

Reading Response Checklist

☐ I started with a thesis statement.

☐ I understand what the question means.

☐ I included three details from the story that support my thesis statement.

☐ My conventions make the piece readable.

Reading Response Checklist

☐ I started with a topic sentence.

☐ I understand what the question means.

☐ I included three details from the story that support my topic sentence.

☐ My conventions make the piece readable.

Reading Response Checklist

☐ I started with a topic sentence.

☐ I understand what the question means.

☐ I included three details from the story that support my topic sentence.

☐ My conventions make the piece readable.

Data Collection 5

The first data chart is designed to show how your individual students are progressing on various questions and texts. It is similar to a grade book.

The Class Summary Data Chart shows how the class is doing altogether. I post this chart so my students can see how they are making progress as a whole. It doesn't show student names, it shows class trends.

The Individual Data Chart is made for students to track their own progress. My students keep this chart in a language arts portfolio binder with the rubric and their responses. They write in the title and date and color in the score they received. This helps them track their individual progress.

Data Collection Chart
Example

Hawai'i Standard: Students will respond to texts from a range of stances: initial understanding, personal, interpretive, and critical.

Hawai'i Benchmark: State the important ideas and interpret author's message, theme, or generalization.

Hawai'i Performance Indicator: The student interprets theme or author's message using specific information from the text to reach conclusions (e.g., citing specific pages in the text to reach a conclusion or conclusions, retelling a part of the text as evidence, reading passages from the text to support statements).

Book Title	Too Much TV, Berenstains	Fine School, Creech				
Question	Author's Message	How did Your Opinion Change?				
Joe	A	M				
Sandy	M	M				
Susan	M	E				
Tanya	N	N				
Eleanor	N	A				
Rob	M	A				
Joanna	E	E				

Data Collection Chart

Standard:

Benchmark:

Performance Indicator:

Book Title						
Question						

Class Summary Data Chart
Example

Book Title	Too Much TV	Fine School											
Question Number	1	1											
Exceeds	1	2											
Meets	3	2											
Approaching	1	2											
Needs Work	2	1											

Class Summary Data Chart

Book Title													
Question Number													
Exceeds													
Meets													
Approaching													
Needs Work													

Individual Data Chart
Example

Title and Date	Too Much TV 12/1	Fine School 1/5										
4												
3												
2												
1												

Individual Data Chart

Title and Date												
4												
3												
2												
1												

Suggested Texts 6

The suggested texts are a mix of chapter books of various reading levels and picture books. When using chapter books, I usually read the first chapter aloud and have the students respond to that. This not only gives the students a chance to respond to the book but it also sparks their interest in those books. In their reading logs, students respond to questions using chapter books that they are reading independently.

Many reading and writing teachers are now seeing the worth of picture books in their classrooms. For the reading response process, picture books are priceless. The story is complete in less than 15 minutes, and books can be chosen with the specific question in mind.

Try out the following questions with their associated titles. The anchor pieces were written using these suggested titles.

Comprehension of Narrative Texts

Question	Title
Point out the main idea of the passage.*	*George Washington's Teeth* by Deborah Chandra and Madeleine Comora (picture book)
How does your understanding of the main character help you predict what he or she will do next?	*The Mouse and the Motorcycle* by Beverly Cleary
Predict what will happen next based on the plot of the story.*	*Stone Fox* by John Reynolds Gardiner
Summarize the story.*	*Chasing Redbird* by Sharon Creech
Identify the main problem in the story.*	*Stone Fox* by John Reynolds Gardiner
Describe the mood.*	*Secret Sacrament* by Sherryl Jordan
Compare the setting in this story with the setting in another story you have read.	*Wild Bog Tea* by Annette LeBox *When I Was Young in the Mountains* by Cynthia Rylant (picture books)
Compare the characters in this story with characters in another story.*	*Thief of Dreams* by Todd Strasser *Cruise Control* by Terry Trueman

*These texts have anchor pieces in Chapter 7.

Application of Narrative Texts

Question	Title
Tell the steps a character takes to solve a problem.*	*Charlotte's Web* by E. B. White
Tell how your prior knowledge helped you understand the story.	*Why Mosquitoes Buzz in People's Ears* by Verna Aardema (picture book)
Describe how the mood changed during the story.	*Sylvester and the Magic Pebble* by William Steig (picture book)
Tell how the main character changed during the story.*	*Holes* by Louis Sachar
Tell about the plot development in the story.	*Raising Dragons* by Jerdine Nolen (picture book)
Why do you think the author wrote this passage?	*Tar Beach* by Faith Ringgold (picture book)

*These texts have anchor pieces in Chapter 7.

Analysis of Narrative Texts

Question	Title
What are the attitudes of the main character?*	*Full House: Stephanie* by Lucinda Thomas
What are the feelings of the main character?*	*Charlie and the Great Glass Elevator* by Roald Dahl
What are the motives of the main character?	*Miss Nelson Is Missing* by James Marshall (picture book)
How are the events in the story like things that have happened to you?	*Johnny Long Legs* by Matt Christopher
Compare the characters in the story with someone you know.*	*Thief of Dreams* by Todd Strasser
How are your feelings similar to or different from the main character's feelings?*	*The Great Gilly Hopkins* by Katherine Paterson
Explain whether you would act the same as the main character.*	*Harry Potter and the Chamber of Secrets* by J. K. Rowling
What part interested you most?	*Zen Shorts* by John J. Muth (picture book)
How does the setting compare with where you live?	*Relatives Came* by Cynthia Rylant (picture book)
Tell about a time when you experienced an incident like the one in the story.*	*The River* by Gary Paulsen
Explain how the author's message connects to your own life.*	*When I Was Young in the Mountains* by Cynthia Rylant (picture book)
Make a list of questions you would like to ask the author.	*Dog Heaven* by Cynthia Rylant (picture book)
What questions would you like to ask the main character?*	*Holes* by Louis Sachar

*These texts have anchor pieces in Chapter 7.

There are many books I recommend for working on *author's message,* which is covered by a question in analysis (Explain how the author's message connects to your own life) as well as in evaluation of narrative texts (What part of the story most shows the author's message?).

The ones that are bold have the most obvious author's messages. These are all picture books.

Amazing Grace by Mary Hoffman

Arthur Writes a Story by Marc Brown

A Fine, Fine School by Sharon Creech

The Berenstain Bears and the Trouble With Friends by Stan and Jan Berenstain

The Berenstain Bears and Too Much TV by Stan and Jan Berenstain

Grandfather's Journey by Allen Say

The Recess Queen by Alexis O'Neill

Tanuki's Gift by Tim Myers

Synthesis of Narrative Texts

Question	Title
What conclusions can you draw about characters in the story?	*Officer Buckle and Gloria* by Peggy Rathman (picture book)
Describe the characters' relationships.*	*Animal Farm* by George Orwell
Write a new ending for this story.*	*On the Far Side of the Mountain* by Jean Craighead George
Identify cause-and-effect relationships in this story.*	*Night John* by Gary Paulsen

*These texts have anchor pieces in Chapter 7.

Evaluation of Narrative Texts

Question	Title
What part of the story most shows the author's message?	*Amazing Grace* by Mary Hoffman (picture book)
How does the author imply the character's attitudes?	*The Great Gracie Chase* by Cynthia Rylant (picture book)
Decide whether the problem and solution are realistic.*	*Alexander and the Terrible, Horrible, No Good, Very Bad Day* by Judith Viorst (picture book)
Is the title a good one? Does it represent the passage well?*	*Arthur and the True Francine* by Marc Brown (picture book)
How did your feelings about the main character change during the story?*	"The Water-Horse of Barra" by Winifred Finlay (short story)
How did the author make you want to keep reading?*	*Holes* by Louis Sachar
Tell how the author created the mood.*	*Amazing Grace* by Mary Hoffman (picture book)
Why did the author write this piece?	*Polar Express* by Chris Van Allsburg (picture book)
If you were the main character, would you want the story to end the way it did?	*The Crane Girl* by Veronika Charles (picture book)
How did the author convey the feelings of the main character?	*Stone Soup* by John J. Muth (picture book)
How effective is the author in his or her choice of words?	*I Will Never Not Ever Eat a Tomato* by Lauren Child (picture book)
How effective is the author in writing dialogue?	*Smoky Night* by Eve Bunting
How effective is the author in describing the setting?	*The Desert Is Theirs* by Byrd Baylor (picture book)
How effective is the author in characterization?*	*Owlbert* by Richard Harris (picture book)
How effective is the author in creating the mood?	*The Wall* by Eve Bunting (picture book)
How effective is the author in the use of text features?	*Looking Out for Sarah* by Glenna Lang (picture book)
Did the sequence of events make sense?	*Red Legs* by Ted Lewin (picture book)
How does the author's choice of setting impact the characters?	*Henry Hikes to Fitchburg* by D. B. Johnson (picture book)

*These texts have anchor pieces in Chapter 7.

Informational and functional texts are easiest to find in textbooks and magazines. I have included a few suggested titles here.

Suggested Informational Texts

Question	Title
What added information would you like to read about?*	*Blast Off to Earth! A Look at Geography* by Lorreen Leedy (picture book)
Draw a conclusion after reading this piece.*	"Persistence," *Highlights for Children*, by Paul Richards (article)
What section of the directions was difficult for you?*	"The Sit Up," *The First Book of Physical Fitness* (p. 9), by John Walsh
Evaluate the usefulness of this piece for learning about the topic.*	*Tom Edison's Bright Ideas* by Jack Keller (picture book)
What text features did the author use to make the passage easier to understand?*	*Rabbits* by Monika Wegler
How accurate is the information in this article?*	*Rabbits* by Monika Wegler

*These texts have anchor pieces in Chapter 7.

Anchor Pieces for Selected Questions 7

During my teacher training, my art professor, Marcia Miller, talked on and on about how important it was to show the students an example of what we wanted them to make.

Either from the fear of seeing 25 carbon copies of my example or lack of time to create the example, or both, I didn't give my students an example of an art project until my second year teaching. I was shocked at how well they did.

They didn't copy and, in fact, expanded on the assignment idea.

It is the same with writing. Make transparencies of the anchor pieces you like. Show the students how a good response looks and sounds.

Chapter 3 includes a lesson plan for using anchor pieces.

Then, when they've gotten good at responding, ask if you can use their responses as anchors. Watch out of the corner of your eye as they sit up taller in their seats and smile.

Anchor Piece Comprehension: Narrative

Question: **Point out the main idea of the passage.**
Title: *George Washington's Teeth* by Deborah Chandra and
        Madeleine Comora

The main idea of this book, George Washington's Teeth was that all of George Washington's teeth fell out. George was born in 1732 and he died in 1799 because there was disease in his gums that caused his death.

George never had wooden teeth, George had hippo's teeth, walrus teeth, elephant teeth, cow and human teeth. I think the author wanted us to discover that just because there is serious disease in your teeth, means you can have death. I also learned that taking care of your teeth is very serious.

Thesis statement is underlined, *details are italicized.*

The main idea of this book, George Washington's Teeth was that all of George Washington's teeth fell out. George was born in 1732 and *he died in 1799 because there was disease in his gums that caused his death.*

George never had wooden teeth, George had hippo's teeth, walrus teeth, elephant teeth, cow and human teeth. I think the author wanted us to discover that just because there is serious disease in your teeth, means you can have death. I also learned that taking care of your teeth is very serious.

Anchor Piece Comprehension: Narrative

Question: **Predict what will happen next based on the plot of the story.**

Title: *Stone Fox* by John Reynolds Gardiner

I predict that when Little Willy's grandfather falls ill he will have to watch the farm for his grandfather and save their farm from the tax collector.

Also, I predict that to make the $500.00 fast Little Willy will go for the National Dogsled Race. Little Willy has to challenge against the best dogsled team in the country. The best dog team has never lost a race in their whole life.

Stone Fox, who is on the best team wants the money too. He wants it, but Little Willy really needs it.

Thesis statement is underlined, *details are italicized.*

I predict that when Little Willy's grandfather falls ill he will have to watch the farm for his grandfather and save their farm from the tax collector.

Also, I predict that to make the *$500.00 fast Little Willy will go for the National Dogsled Race. Little Willy has to challenge against the best dogsled team in the country. The best dog team has never lost a race in their whole life.*

Stone Fox, who is on the best team wants the money too. He wants it, but Little Willy really needs it.

Anchor Piece Comprehension: Narrative

Question: **Summarize the story.**
Title: *Chasing Redbird* by Sharon Creech

This story, <u>Chasing Redbird</u>, was about a girl named Rose and another girl named Zinny.

Rose got sick and died. Her mom, Aunt Jessie, put Rose in the dresser drawer and they buried her. Zinny thought she was Rose because everyone was calling her Rose and she's the one that made Rose sick. So it was kind of Zinny's fault that Rose died.

Zinny noticed that all of Rose's things were gone and it was like nobody remembered her but Zinny did. She visited her grave, brought flowers and talked to her.

I think that Zinny really cared for Rose and will always remember her.

<u>Thesis statement is underlined,</u> *details are italicized.*

<u>This story, Chasing Redbird, was about a girl named Rose and another girl named Zinny.</u>
Rose got sick and died. Her mom, Aunt Jessie, put Rose in the dresser drawer and they buried her. Zinny thought she was Rose because everyone was calling her Rose and she's the one that made Rose sick. So it was kind of Zinny's fault that Rose died.

Zinny noticed that all of Rose's things were gone and it was like nobody remembered her but Zinny did. She visited her grave, brought flowers and talked to her.

I think that Zinny really cared for Rose and will always remember her.

Anchor Piece Comprehension: Narrative

Question: **Identify the main problem in the story.**
Title: *Stone Fox* by John Reynolds Gardiner

The story is about a boy whose grandfather becomes very ill. He tries to save the potato farm from the tax collector. He has to raise five hundred dollars. To do that he has to enter the National Dogsled Race. He has to race against the best dogsled team in the country who have never lost a race.

The main problem in the story is that Little Willy's grandfather is very ill and he has to pay five hundred dollars to the tax collector. Another problem is part of the solution. To win the race and get the five hundred dollars, Little Willy has to race against the best dogsled team in the country.

Thesis statement is underlined, *details are italicized.*

The story is about a boy whose grandfather becomes very ill. He tries to save the potato farm from the tax collector. He has to raise five hundred dollars. To do that he has to enter the National Dogsled Race. He has to race against the best dogsled team in the country who have never lost a race.

The main problem in the story is that Little Willy's grandfather is very ill and he has to pay five hundred dollars to the tax collector. *Another problem is part of the solution. To win the race and get the five hundred dollars, Little Willy has to race against the best dogsled team in the country.*

Anchor Piece Comprehension: Narrative

Question: **Describe the mood.**
Title: *Secret Sacrament* by Sherryl Jordan

"In perfect harmony he worked with Salverion, intuitively knowing what the surgeon wanted and when he wanted it, his motions swift and sure." (page 77) This is part of the author's description of Gabriel's first assistance with surgery. At first it shows Gabriel's anxiety but as the procedure starts, he becomes confident and does a great job. This stretch of the story continues, briefly informing you of Gabriel's new routine at the Citidale and his practices.

The quote I selected, in my opinion, gives you the mood and feeling of how the surgeon and is assistant go through their procedure. It shows you confidence, cooperation and most of all, a sense of tenderness and caring from the operators towards the patient. It also gives you the felling of trust between them.

Anchor Piece Comprehension: Narrative

Question: **Compare the characters in this story with characters in another story you have read.**
Title: *The Thief of Dreams* by Todd Strasser and *Cruise Control* by Terry Trueman

The character in <u>Cruise Control,</u> Paul, and Martin in <u>Thief of Dreams</u> are alike because they both aren't afraid to do things. Martin is more sneaky and the Paul is always grouchy.

Martin lives with his parents and Paul lives with his mother and has a bad relationship with his dad.

Anchor Piece Application: Narrative

Question: **Tell the steps the character takes to solve a problem.**
Title: *Charlotte's Web* by E. B. White

The first step Fern did to save Wilbur is that one morning Fern's father was going to kill Wilbur so Fern said, "You can not kill this little poor piglet."

The second step Fern did was take a bottle and feed the little piglet so she can make the little piglet live.

The third step Fern did was take good care of the piglet that is really young. The fourth step Fern did was to go to the barn of her uncle and see Wilbur whenever she could.

Fern was the first one to save Wilbur's life, Charlotte was the second.

Anchor Piece Application: Narrative

Question: **Tell how the main character changed during the story.**
Title: *Holes* by Louis Sachar

Zero changed by becoming more responsible and telling the truth. Zero tells the truth because when he and Stanley were at the big thumb he said to Stanley that if he didn't steal the shoes they wouldn't be here right now.

Then Stanley said, "Oh, Clyde Livingston's shoes?" And Zero said, Yes, I stole them, so you're innocent and then Zero told Stanley how he saw them at the shelter and how he threw them over the overpass. That's why it hit Stanley on the head and that's why he got arrested because Clyde thought he stole it. But if I were Zero, I would have done the same thing and told Stanley the truth.

Anchor Piece Analysis: Narrative

Question: **What are the attitudes of the main character?**
Title: *Full House: Stephanie* by Lucinda Thomas

The attitudes of the main character are shown mostly in how she acts to her father. Stephanie fights with her father because he treats her like a baby. He does things for her and she feels like she has an overprotective dad. But she also feels lucky to have a dad like him.

Anchor Piece Analysis: Narrative

Question: **What are the feelings of the main character?**
Title: *Charlie and the Great Glass Elevator* by Roald Dahl

In this part of the book, Charlie is starting to feel worried about Mr. Wonka. He feels worried because in the middle of the book they are still up in space. Charlie thought they were going to die from the knids because a lot of knids were coming after them. Then he also felt worried at the end of the story because Mr. Wonka gave the four grandparents some kind of vitamin to make them younger so when grandma Georgina took the vitamin, she disappeared. Charlie got more worried because he thought he wasn't going to see his grandma again.

Anchor Piece Analysis: Narrative

Question: **Compare the characters in the story with someone you know.**
Title: *Thief of Dreams* by Todd Strasser

The main character, Martin, is a person that is friendly but has to find out things and can't mind his own business. Sometimes Martin feels worried that his uncle won't come home but other than that he's happy.

Martin and my sister are alike because they both get along with our uncles and they both have to find things out.

Anchor Piece Analysis: Narrative

Question: **How are your feelings similar to or different from the main character's feelings?**
Title: *The Great Gilly Hopkins* by Katherine Paterson

My feelings compared to Gilly's feelings but Gilly's feelings are stronger than mine.

Gilly's feelings are that she's feeling stubborn, like she doesn't want to do something. Sometimes I don't want to do anything either.

Gilly was going to a foster home when she didn't want to go. I felt like that once, a little. I felt like my mom was going to kick me out of the house and I was going to become a foster child. My mom was so mad at me that she said, "You are going to leave this house with no clothes, just the clothes on your back!"

Another feeling that she had was that everyone was calling her Gilly instead of her real name. I felt like that when my uncle and my mom called me by my nicknames.

Gilly and I are alike because our lives relate to each other. We are like soulmates or best friends.

Anchor Piece Analysis: Narrative

Question: **Explain whether you would act the same as the main character.**
Title: *Harry Potter and the Chamber of Secrets* by J. K. Rowling

I am still reading Harry Potter and the Chamber of Secrets by J. K. Rowling. I would not act the way Harry did because if people were thinking I was the heir of Slitherin I would take advantage of that and start freaking out every one that I ran into on the corridors, in the Great Hall and by the lake. I wouldn't try to explain like Harry did.

Anchor Piece Analysis: Narrative

Question: **Tell about a time when you experienced an incident like the one in the story.**
Title: *The River* by Gary Paulsen

I didn't experience an incident like the one in the story, but my dad did.

Brian saved a guy in the story and my dad saved a guy too.

My dad was surfing and this guy went scuba diving. A set of waves came in and the man didn't have any control of his swimming. He got tired and couldn't swim back to shore. He called for help and my dad heard someone calling and looked toward the sound. He saw that the man was drowning.

My dad swam to him with his surfboard and grabbed him by his arm and pulled him onto the surfboard. Then my dad brought him safely to the shore. The man didn't even say thanks.

This incident was a lot like when Brian saved the man in the story because the man and Brian didn't get along.

Anchor Piece Analysis: Narrative

Question: **Explain how the author's message connects to your own life.**

Title: *When I Was Young in the Mountains* by Cynthia Rylant

I think the author's message is about the mountain that they lived in and had fun on. Once when I was small and I went to visit my grandfather and my grandmother up the mountains. Instead of swimming with muddy dirty water I swam in a hot spring. I didn't get enough sleep because my grandmother's cat made big noise chasing rats. So this one night I opened the window and got my pellet gun and shot a big rat. Then I gave the rat to the cat and he ate. The next day me and my grandfather went to go hunting. And you know what we saw, I saw a big boar. That its belly almost touched the ground. My grandfather shot it the same time and dragged it back to his house. I ate a lot that night. I love the mountain. When I grow up I'm going to live up there. I think she loves the mountain. The author wrote this story because he might have lived up mountain before. That's what I think his author's message is about.

Anchor Piece Analysis: Narrative

Question: **Make a list of questions that you would like to ask the main character.**

Title: *Holes* by Louis Sachar

I am still reading Holes and I would like to ask Stanley why he thought the shoes were his family's destiny? Also I would like to ask Hector (Zero) why he stole the shoes. Why did he throw them away from him when he needed shoes? Where did Stanley live?

Anchor Piece Analysis: Informational

Question: **What added information would you like to read about?**
Title: *Blast Off to Earth! A Look at Geography* by Loreen Leedy

I learned about the land masses that have many continents. I would love to learn more about the temperatures around the whole world. I found out that the earth is covered mostly with water. These facts interest me because I can learn more about the earth, its land masses and continents. The thing that I want to learn more specifically is why doesn't the earth melt if the inside is over 1,000,000 degrees?

I also want to know why the Great Wall of China is in Asia. Why don't they call it the Great Wall of Asia? Why are the best animals in Africa?

Anchor Piece Analysis: Informational

Question: **Draw a conclusion after reading this piece.**
Title: "Persistence" by Paul Richards

I learned that when you win something you have to take time making what you want to win with. Ok, say you want to win a horse race. Do you beat the horse? No. You have to take time.

In this article, Paul Richards wants to be an astronaut. He went to school to be an astronaut. Then he waited for eight years. Two more years and he'll be going to school as long as I've been alive.

But the main point is that he never gave up because he was determined to be an astronaut and in those eight years he got rejected. But he finally got accepted to Houston, Texas where he was launched on the "Discovery" into space. He worked in space for twelve days. In all, he was in space for 307 hours.

He wouldn't have been there if he hadn't had persistence. That is the conclusion I drew.

Anchor Piece Analysis: Functional

Question: **What section of the directions was difficult for you?**

Title: "Sit Ups," in *Physical Fitness, President's Council on Physical Fitness*

Three of the directions were hard for me to follow because they were confusing.

The direction that was difficult for me was the part that says sitting erect. That part is hard for me because I don't know what erect means.

The other difficult direction is to fall back slowly because what if you hurt yourself? Maybe it should say to slowly lay back down to a flat position.

The last direction that was hard for me was hook your toes under something because the word hook makes it confusing. I think it should be written like this, then put your toes under something heavy.

The rest of the directions were easy to follow.

Anchor Piece Synthesis: Narrative

Question: **Describe the character's relationships.**

Title: *Animal Farm* by George Orwell

The relationship among the pigs and the rest of the animals on the farm is like a dictatorship. All animals were made equal after the rebellion, but now Napoleon is referred to as "our Leader, Comrade Napoleon," page 90.

One example of this is how he and the pigs now live in perfect human luxury where every other animal sleeps in their stalls. He has dictated their time to make a windmill. It has been built, destroyed, built again even stronger and destroyed again. Rumors are constantly being spread or made up.

I think Napoleon has been planting those lies in order to sway the opinion of the others towards his wanting.

Anchor Piece Synthesis: Narrative

Question: **Write a new ending for the story.**
Title: *On the Far Side of the Mountain* by Jean Craighead George

I have now finished On the Far Side of the Mountain and I think that another good ending for this story would be:

I was by this huge waterfall with my new goshawk because I just got my falcon/hawk permit and I started to whistle. All of a sudden, I saw Fightfull, my old bird. Now I have all that I want.

Anchor Piece Synthesis: Narrative

Question: **Identify cause-and-effect relationships in this story.**
Title: *On Night John* by Gary Paulsen

The cause in this book is that John taught a girl how to read and a man caught the girl, but the girl did not tell the truth.

The effect is that the girl's mom got dragged by the man that caught John and the girl reading. The man whipped the girl's mom until her back was covered with bloody lines.

Because John taught the girl to read, her mother got beaten. That is the cause and the effect.

Anchor Piece Evaluation: Narrative

Question: **Decide whether the problem and solution are realistic.**

Title: *Alexander and the Terrible, Horrible, No Good, Very Bad Day* by Judith Viorst

I agree that Alexander's problems might happen because before I had a terrible day. I had a bad hair day, dress in funny different clothes, like different kinds of colors. Yes, it could happen like when I went to Hilo one time I was looking at a phone. In Sears I puted it back then accedently elbowed another phone. Then phones all started to fall and I was trying to catch all of them. I puted them back then I started to walk. I banged into a pole where they hang the clothes then I went into the car and smashed my finger. I went to Walmart I steped on gum my feet got stuck. I went to eat at mcdonald's I got ketchup on my shirt then my nephew flyed mushed up French fries in my hair. Yes, the problem and solution are realistic because I had a really bad day.

Anchor Piece Evaluation: Narrative

Question: **Is the title a good one? Does it represent the passage well?**

Title: *Arthur and the True Francine* by Marc Brown

I think the title isn't good because it was about Muffy cheating and lieing, not really about the true francine. All we know about Francine is that she studeyed and she got in trouble, I mean, a lot of trouble, because Muffy lied and said should never cheat on a test. So Francine has to clean the class room and she has a game in three days. Finally, Muffy told Mr. Ratburn/teacher about she lieing and everything so Francine was able to go to the game and she one the game with a home run and thats what I think.

Marc Brown should change the title because it doesn't really tell you that the story will be about Francine getting in trouble for something that she didn't do.

Anchor Piece Evaluation: Narrative

Question: **How did your feelings about the main character change during the story?**
Title: "The Water-Horse of Barra," *Junior Great Books Series 4*, by Winifred Finlay

My feelings about the main character changed a little.
I thought he was going to get a really good wife and he did.
My opinion that he was going to stay a horse changed. Instead, he drank a potion that took his magic out and because he didn't have his magic, he stayed a man and couldn't go back to being a horse.
I thought the water horse would stay as a water horse.
My thoughts changed and so did the water horse's life.
I predict that he will still visit the lake where he used to live and probably fish there.

Anchor Piece Evaluation: Narrative

Question: **How did the author make you want to keep reading?**
Title: *Holes* by Louis Sachar

The author made me want to keep reading by building suspense. In one part of the story Stanley found a tube that looked goldish and had someone's initials on it. So the author made me want to keep reading because I wanted to see what Stanley was going to do with it.
I wanted to see if he was going to show it to the warden and get the rest of the day off. Or maybe he would give it to X-Ray so X-Ray could get the day off. X-Ray told Stanley that if he found anything while he was digging to give it to him because X-Ray was at Camp Green Lake for one year and he wanted to take a day off.

Anchor Piece Evaluation: Narrative

Question: **Tell how the author created the mood.**
Title: *Amazing Grace* by Mary Hoffman

The author created the mood by showing how sad Grace felt when her class discussed the Peter Pan play.

Grace feels sad because her class was doing a Peter Pan play and everyone wanted to be Peter Pan. Raj said that Grace is a girl and girls can't be Peter Pan.

Then Natalie said that Grace is black and that Peter Pan has to be white.

Grace was sad but she stilled raised her hand to be Peter Pan. The author showed how Grace felt.

In the beginning of the story she was happy but when it go to the middle when they were at school she was sad.

Anchor Piece Evaluation: Narrative

Question: **How effective is the author in characterization?**
Title: *Owlbert* by Richard Harris

Mr. Harris created Nicholas to be a boy that loved to have pets but his parents kept saying no. Mr. Harris explained why the parents said no. When Nicholas asked if he could have a pet bird, a pet dog and pet mice, his parents said no. Nicholas still didn't get a pet.

If I was the author I would represent Nicholas to be similar to how he is, but I would describe more about Nicholas. I would explain more about how Nicholas felt about finding the dead owl, it's baby and how he felt while he was taking care of the baby so it wouldn't die.

Mr. Harris did a good job on creating the characters, but he could have explained their feelings more.

Anchor Piece Evaluation: Narrative

Question: **Is the setting realistic or fantastic?**
Title: *The Catcher in the Rye* by J. D. Salinger

The Catcher in the Rye is a fictional book but it is not fantasy in any way. It is all based on events that could definitely happen in New York City. The author makes this situation real by giving examples of real things in the setting.

There was graffiti written with red crayon under the glass part of the wall. This makes the story real because in real life we have graffiti. Some kids get a kick out of doing this. I don't think its really funny.

Anchor Piece Evaluation: Narrative

Question: **Are the characters realistic?**
Title: *Harry Potter and the Goblet of Fire* by J. K. Rowling

J. K. Rowling made this book seem very real by making very realistic characters.

Harry being an orphan is a good example. I actually have a friend who lost both of her parents in a car accident and was forced to live with her awful aunt.

Another example would be the attraction between Ron and Hermonie. Seeing as they are best friends, its only obvious that they would be somewhat attracted to each other. I have been through the same situation where I was attracted to my close guy friends.

"Just because its taken you three years to notice, Ron, doesn't mean no one else has spotted I'm a girl!" (page 400)

Lastly, jealousy! In this story Harry tends to face a lot of jealousy towards fellow Quidditch players who will get more attention. Everyone knows that they are jealous of someone who gets more attention, its only natural.

"Now he realized that Cedric was in fact a useless pretty boy who didn't have enough brains to fill an egg cup." (page 398)

Anchor Piece Evaluation: Narrative

Question: **How did the author make the story seem like it could really happen?**
Title: *Harry Potter and the Goblet of Fire* by J. K. Rowling

The author, J. K. Rowling, makes the story seem like it could happen in many ways. She likes to relate the characters to real life scenarios. For instance, the characters have to deal with teen relationships, hormones and education.

A good example is in this particular chapter. They are planning to have a formal dance where the teen boys have to ask the girls, just like in real life high school.

Even in the story, the boys and girls go through rejection. On page 397,

"D'you- d'you want to go to the ball with me?" Harry asked.

"Oh Harry, I'm really sorry, I've already said I'd go with someone else!"

Harry actually shows his basic boyish awkwardness by cluelessly and somewhat coldly rebuffing several girls who ask him to the dance. He then makes himself vulnerable by asking Cho, but finds out that she already has a date! I think its awesome that the author can make this seem so real, seeing as it relates so well to teenagers these days!

Anchor Piece Evaluation: Informational

Question: **Evaluate the usefulness of this piece for learning about the topic.**
Title: *Tom Edison's Bright Ideas* by Jack Keller

This book, <u>Tom Edison's Bright Ideas,</u> is useful because you know if you wanted to do a project about Thomas Edison you could look in this book.

Thomas liked to do experiments and his mom built him a lab. Thomas liked to invent things.

If I was writing a report on Thomas Edison, I would use this book to find out about him sitting on goose eggs. I could use this book to read about how Thomas got interested in light and lightening. I found out about how Thomas invented the light bulb and started inventing other things.

Anchor Piece Evaluation: Informational

Question: **What text features did the author use to make the passage easier to understand?**
Title: *Rabbits* by Monika Wegler

The subtitles and pictures in this article make it easier to read. The part about nail clipping was very interesting because we had to clip the nails of my guinea pig.

The part of the article where they talked about grooming has a good subtitle and pictures that are great.

Now I know to draw interesting pictures when I write an article.

Anchor Piece Evaluation: Informational

Question: **How accurate is the information in this article?**
Title: "Handling," in *Rabbits,* by Monika Wegler

The accuracy of this article is very on target I think that it is correct because in the article it say to never pick up the rabbit by its ears. Well, that I now know is true because before we used to have rabbits an I picked it up by the ears and it died. My aunty scolded me then I had to go and get the other rabbit and I picked it up exactly how it says in the article. And luckily, that rabbit did not die. It said to hold the extra skin on the neck and put your hand under the butt. And the rabbit did stay calm when I picked it up and the article was correct it will stay calm.

Anchor Piece Evaluation: Functional

Question: **Do you have to do the steps in order?**
Title: Multistep math problem

No, you don't have to follow the steps in order because you can do step two and then step one. But you will always do step three last because if you would have to draw the pictures to make it easier. Also because if you do step three and then step one and two then you probably wouldn't know what they were talking about. If you drew the pictures last it probably would be clear to you.

Independent Reading Logs 8

I've included all the reading response questions that relate to narrative texts in the reading log lists. Most students read novels for their independent reading. If that is not the case in your class, or you would like your students to practice responding to informational or functional texts, make lists using those questions.

There is a section of questions for each level of Bloom's Taxonomy, so you may want to use the first section in the first weeks of school and so on.

If your students are more advanced, you may want to have them work on the last section all year.

The important thing I find about reading logs is that the students need to feel that they matter. I check everyone's log for completion every morning. When I have a class of 25, I collect five logs a day to read when I have a chance. If you don't have time during the day to read five logs, you could read them after school and give those five students no reading log that night or an alternative assignment. It is very important to read the logs and respond with feedback and suggestions.

You may want to have your students choose a piece from their reading logs to include in their language arts portfolio.

Reading Log Questions

Comprehension of Narrative Texts

1. Point out the main idea of the passage.

2. How does your understanding of the main character help you predict what he or she will do next?

3. Predict what will happen next based on the plot of the story.

4. Summarize the story.

5. Identify the main problem in the story.

6. Describe the mood.

7. Compare the setting of this story with the setting of another story you have read.

8. Compare the characters in this story with the characters in another story you have read.

Application of Narrative Texts

9. Tell the steps a character takes to solve a problem.

10. Tell how your prior knowledge helped you understand the story.

11. Describe how the mood changed during the story.

12. Tell how the main character changed during the story.

13. Tell about the plot development in the story.

14. Why do you think the author wrote this passage?

Analysis of Narrative Texts

15. How are the events in the story like things that have happened to you?

16. Compare the characters in the story with someone you know.

17. How are your feelings similar to or different from the main character's feelings?

18. Explain whether you would act the same as the main character.

19. Which part interested you most?

20. How does the setting compare with where you live?

21. Tell about a time when you experienced an incident like the one in the story.

22. Explain how the author's message connects to your own life.

23. Make a list of questions you would like to ask the author.

24. What questions would you like to ask the main character?

25. What are the attitudes of the main character?

26. What are the feelings of the main character?

27. What are the motives of the main character?

Synthesis of Narrative Texts

28. What conclusions can you draw about characters in the story?

29. Describe the characters' relationships.

30. Write a new ending for this story.

31. Identify cause-and-effect relationships in this story.

Evaluation of Narrative Texts

32. What part of the story best shows the author's message?

33. How does the author imply the character's attitudes?

34. Decide whether the problem and solution are realistic.

35. Is the title a good one? Does it represent the passage well?

36. How did your feelings about the main character change during the story?

37. How did the author make you want to keep reading?

38. Tell how the author created the mood.

39. Why did the author write this piece?

40. If you were the main character, would you want the story to end the way it did?

41. How did the author convey the feelings of the main character?

42. How effective is the author in his or her word choice?

43. How effective is the author in writing dialogue?

44. How effective is the author in describing the setting?

45. How effective is the author in characterization?

46. How effective is the author in creating the mood?

47. How effective is the author in the use of text features?

48. Did the sequence of events make sense?

49. How does the author's choice of setting impact the characters?

50. Is the setting realistic or fantastic?

51. How does the author show that the story is fantasy?

52. Are the characters realistic?

53. How did the author make the story seem like it could happen?

SECTION 2

Comprehension

(An Understanding of What Was Read)

Comprehension of Narrative Texts 9

Name _____   **Comprehension: Narrative**

Point out the main idea of the passage.

Vocabulary Box

point out	identify, show, choose
main idea	what the book is about, main point, what you learned
passage	book, text, or article

Student-Friendly Translation

Point out what you learned from the book.

This means:

What did you learn from the book? What was the book mostly about?
What did the author want you to discover by reading this book? Use details from the story to explain your ideas!

Write, write, write, explain, explain, explain!

Name _____   **Comprehension: Narrative**

Point out the main idea of the passage.

Vocabulary Box

point out	
main idea	
passage	

Student-Friendly Translation

Point out what you learned from the book.

This means:

What did you learn from the book? What was the book mostly about?

What did the author want you to discover by reading this book? Use details from the story to explain your ideas!

Write, write, write, explain, explain, explain!

Name _____ **Comprehension: Narrative**

How does your understanding of the main character help you predict what he or she will do next?

Vocabulary Box

understanding	knowledge, insight, what you know about
main character	the most important person in the passage
predict	make a guess, imagine what will happen

Student-Friendly Translation

> How does your knowledge about the most important person in the story help you guess what will happen next?

This means:

> What do you think will happen next in the story? Think about the main character and what he or she has done already. Use that information to guess what will happen next. Your prediction must make sense based on the story. Use details from the story to show why you think that will happen.

Write, write, write, explain, explain, explain!

Name _____   **Comprehension: Narrative**

How does your understanding of the main character help you predict what he or she will do next?

Vocabulary Box

understanding	
main character	
predict	

Student-Friendly Translation

> How does your knowledge about the most important person in the story help you guess what will happen next?

This means:

> What do you think will happen next in the story? Think about the main character and what he or she has done already. Use that information to guess what will happen next. Your prediction must make sense based on the story. Use details from the story to show why you think that will happen.

Write, write, write, explain, explain, explain!

Name _____   **Comprehension: Narrative**

Predict what will happen next based on the plot of the story.

Vocabulary Box

predict what will happen next	imagine, make an educated guess
based on the plot of the story	thinking of the story, considering what has happened in the story

Student-Friendly Translation

Based on what has happened so far in the story, give details about what you think will happen next.

This means:

Make an educated guess or prediction using the information from the story. Be sure to give details from the story to support your ideas. Remember, you must talk about the problem, solution, or events of the story to support your ideas.

Write, write, write, explain, explain, explain!

Name _____   **Comprehension: Narrative**

Predict what will happen next based on the plot of the story.

Vocabulary Box

predict what will happen next	
based on the plot of the story	

Student-Friendly Translation

Based on what has happened so far in the story, give details about what you think will happen next.

This means:

Make an educated guess or prediction using the information from the story. Be sure to give details from the story to support your ideas. Remember, you must talk about the problem, solution, or events of the story to support your ideas.

Write, write, write, explain, explain, explain!

Name _____   **Comprehension: Narrative**

Summarize the story.

Vocabulary Box

summarize	go over the main points, sum up, recap
the story	the selection, passage, book

Student-Friendly Translation

Go over the main points in the passage.

This means:

Think about the main characters. Think about the setting. Think about the main things that happened in the story. Write a short summary of what happened in the story. Don't tell small details. Example: In *Little Red Riding Hood,* a little girl goes to visit her grandmother. A wolf tries to trick her so he can eat her. She figures out who he is and rescues her grandmother.

Write, write, write, explain, explain, explain!

Comprehension

Name _____   **Comprehension: Narrative**

Summarize the story.

Vocabulary Box

summarize	
the story	

Student-Friendly Translation

Go over the main points in the passage.

This means:

Think about the main characters. Think about the setting. Think about the main things that happened in the story. Write a short summary of what happened in the story. Don't tell small details. Example: In *Little Red Riding Hood,* a little girl goes to visit her grandmother. A wolf tries to trick her so he can eat her. She figures out who he is and rescues her grandmother.

Write, write, write, explain, explain, explain!

Name _____   **Comprehension: Narrative**

Identify the main problem in the story.

Vocabulary Box

identify	name, discover, spot, point out
main	major, most important
problem	what the characters have to solve, difficulty

Student-Friendly Translation

Point out the most important difficulty that has to be solved in the story.

This means:

Every story has a problem and a solution. The problem could be as small as a lost pencil or as large as a lost child. Some stories have many problems. What is the main problem in this selection? Find the most important problem and explain how you know it is the main problem with details from the selection.

Write, write, write, explain, explain, explain!

Name _____   **Comprehension: Narrative**

Identify the main problem in the story.

Vocabulary Box

identify	
main	
problem	

Student-Friendly Translation

> Point out the most important difficulty that has to be solved in the story.

This means:

> Every story has a problem and a solution. The problem could be as small as a lost pencil or as large as a lost child. Some stories have many problems. What is the main problem in this selection? Find the most important problem and explain how you know it is the main problem with details from the selection.

Write, write, write, explain, explain, explain!

Name _____   **Comprehension: Narrative**

Describe the mood.

Vocabulary Box

describe	explain, tell about, give details
mood	atmosphere, feeling, vibes, tone

Student-Friendly Translation

Tell about the general feeling of the passage. Give details
from the passage!

This means:

Would you call this a sad book? Or a happy, joyous, exciting book? Or is
it a scary book? What is the general feeling of the story? Use details
from the passage to explain the mood that you have chosen.

Write, write, write, explain, explain, explain!

Name _____   **Comprehension: Narrative**

Describe the mood.

Vocabulary Box

describe	
mood	

Student-Friendly Translation

Tell about the general feeling of the passage. Give details from the passage!

This means:

Would you call this a sad book? Or a happy, joyous, exciting book? Or is it a scary book? What is the general feeling of the story? Use details from the passage to explain the mood that you have chosen.

Write, write, write, explain, explain, explain!

Name _____ **Comprehension: Narrative**

Compare the setting of this story with the setting of another story you have read.

Vocabulary Box

compare	tell how they are the same and different
setting	main place and time period of the story

Student-Friendly Translation

Tell how the main place and time period in the story are the same or different from the main place and time period in another story. Explain using the details of the stories.

This means:

Think about the main places and time periods in both stories. Do the two stories take place in similar places? Time periods can be difficult to figure out. Do the stories take place in the past, present, or future? Some stories are based on historical time periods like the Civil War, the colonial period, or the 1960s. How are the places and time periods alike? How are they different? Use the details from the stories to explain your ideas.

Write, write, write, explain, explain, explain!

Name _____   **Comprehension: Narrative**

Compare the setting of this story with the setting of another story you have read.

Vocabulary Box

compare	
setting	

Student-Friendly Translation

> Tell how the main place and time period in the story are the same or different from the main place and time period in another story. Explain using the details of the stories.

This means:

> Think about the main places and time periods in both stories. Do the two stories take place in similar places? Time periods can be difficult to figure out. Do the stories take place in the past, present, or future? Some stories are based on historical time periods like the Civil War, the colonial period, or the 1960s. How are the places and time periods alike? How are they different? Use the details from the stories to explain your ideas.

Write, write, write, explain, explain, explain!

Name _____   **Comprehension: Narrative**

Compare the characters in this story with the characters in another story you have read.

Vocabulary Box

compare	tell how they are the same and different
characters	people or animals in the story

Student-Friendly Translation

Tell how the people (or animals) in the story are the same as or different from the people (or animals) in another story. Explain using the details of the stories.

This means:

Think about the main people (or animals) in both stories. Think of their personal qualities. Are they both brave or patient or kind? How are they alike? How are they different? Use the details from the stories to explain your ideas

Write, write, write, explain, explain, explain!

Name _____   **Comprehension: Narrative**

Compare the characters in this story with the characters in another story you have read.

Vocabulary Box

compare	
characters	

Student-Friendly Translation

> Tell how the people (or animals) in the story are the same as or different from the people (or animals) in another story. Explain using the details of the stories.

This means:

> Think about the main people (or animals) in both stories. Think of their personal qualities. Are they both brave or patient or kind? How are they alike? How are they different? Use the details from the stories to explain your ideas

Write, write, write, explain, explain, explain!

Comprehension of 10
Informational Texts

Name _____   **Comprehension: Informational**

Tell what someone who read this article would learn from reading it.

Vocabulary Box

tell	explain, give details, point out
someone who read this article	you or any one else who reads this selection, the reader

Student-Friendly Translation

> Explain what the reader of this passage (you!) can learn from it. Look at the facts or new understandings you have from this passage.

This means:

> What did you learn? If someone else read it, what would he or she learn? What information did you find out about in the passage? Be sure to include details from the passage!

Write, write, write, explain, explain, explain!

Name _____   **Comprehension: Informational**

Tell what someone who read this article would learn from reading it.

Vocabulary Box

tell	
someone who read this article	

Student-Friendly Translation

> Explain what the reader of this passage (you!) can learn from it. Look at the facts or new understandings you have from this passage.

This means:

> What did you learn? If someone else read it, what would he or she learn? What information did you find out about in the passage? Be sure to include details from the passage!

Write, write, write, explain, explain, explain!

Name _____   **Comprehension: Informational**

Restate the information from this piece.

Vocabulary Box

restate	repeat in your own words, paraphrase
information	facts, knowledge
piece	passage, selection, article

Student-Friendly Translation

Tell the information from the passage in your own words.

This means:

Think about what you read or heard. Tell that information in your own words. Be sure to tell about at least three details. Be sure to use YOUR OWN WORDS!

Write, write, write, explain, explain, explain!

Name _____   **Comprehension: Informational**

Restate the information from this piece.

Vocabulary Box

restate	
information	
piece	

Student-Friendly Translation

Tell the information from the passage in your own words.

This means:

Think about what you read or heard. Tell that information in your own words. Be sure to tell about at least three details. Be sure to use YOUR OWN WORDS!

Write, write, write, explain, explain, explain!

Name _____   **Comprehension: Informational**

Name details from this selection that support the main idea.

Vocabulary Box

name	quote, cite, mention
details	facts, information, particulars
support	give more information about
main idea	main point, topic, subject

Student-Friendly Translation

Name the facts that give more information about the topic.

This means:

Figure out what the topic of the passage is. Every sentence in the passage should give information about it if it is the main topic. Then look for details that tell more about that topic. Write them down. Be sure to write clearly and include at least three details.

Write, write, write, explain, explain, explain!

Name _____   **Comprehension: Informational**

Name details from this selection that support the main idea.

Vocabulary Box

name	
details	
support	
main idea	

Student-Friendly Translation

Name the facts that give more information about the topic.

This means:

Figure out what the topic of the passage is. Every sentence in the passage should give information about it if it is the main topic. Then look for details that tell more about that topic. Write them down. Be sure to write clearly and include at least three details.

Write, write, write, explain, explain, explain!

Name _____ **Comprehension: Informational**

Make a prediction about the course of action the author may take next.

Vocabulary Box

make a prediction	make an educated guess, figure out, describe
course of action	what will happen, what someone will do, path
author	the person who wrote this passage

Student-Friendly Translation

Figure out what the author will do next.

This means:

Think about what you know about the author from what you read here. Think about what you know about the information in the passage. What do you think the author will or should do next? A good answer would consider the author's views and opinions on the subject of the passage. Be sure to include details from the passage that gave you these ideas.

Write, write, write, explain, explain, explain!

Name _____   **Comprehension: Informational**

Make a prediction about the course of action the author may take next.

Vocabulary Box

make a prediction	
course of action	
author	

Student-Friendly Translation

Figure out what the author will do next.

This means:

Think about what you know about the author from what you read here. Think about what you know about the information in the passage. What do you think the author will or should do next? A good answer would consider the author's views and opinions on the subject of the passage. Be sure to include details from the passage that gave you these ideas.

Write, write, write, explain, explain, explain!

Name _____   **Comprehension: Informational**

Use your prior knowledge to predict what information will be next.

Vocabulary Box

prior knowledge	what you already know, everything you have learned or experienced in your life
predict	make an educated guess, figure out
what information will be next	what facts will be written about next, what knowledge will be next in the passage

Student-Friendly Translation

> Give examples of what you know about the topic that help you figure out what facts will be next in the passage. Use details from the passage to explain your ideas.

This means:

> Imagine this passage was part of a book. What would you expect to read about next? Why? Tell what you know about the subject of this passage that helps you decide what would be next. Remember to use details from the passage!

Write, write, write, explain, explain, explain!

Name _____   **Comprehension: Informational**

Use your prior knowledge to predict what information will be next.

Vocabulary Box

prior knowledge	
predict	
what information will be next	

Student-Friendly Translation

Give examples of what you know about the topic that help you figure out what facts will be next in the passage. Use details from the passage to explain your ideas.

This means:

Imagine this passage was part of a book. What would you expect to read about next? Why? Tell what you know about the subject of this passage that helps you decide what would be next. Remember to use details from the passage!

Write, write, write, explain, explain, explain!

Name _____   **Comprehension: Informational**

Point out the most important section.

Vocabulary Box

point out	identify, name, spot, discover
most important	key, main, significant
section	part, piece

Student-Friendly Translation

Name the main part. Give details to show why you think it is important.

This means:

What is the most significant or important part of the passage? Which part could you not take out? Explain why you think so, using details from the passage.

Write, write, write, explain, explain, explain!

Name _____ **Comprehension: Informational**

Point out the most important section.

Vocabulary Box

point out	
most important	
section	

Student-Friendly Translation

Name the main part. Give details to show why you think it is important.

This means:

What is the most significant or important part of the passage? Which part could you not take out? Explain why you think so, using details from the passage.

Write, write, write, explain, explain, explain!

Name _____   **Comprehension: Informational**

Compare information from this passage to information from another passage.

Vocabulary Box

compare	tell what is alike and different
information	facts, knowledge
passage	article, piece, selection, or book

Student-Friendly Translation

> Tell what is the same and what is different about the facts from this article and another you have read. Use details from the passage to explain your ideas.

This means:

> Think carefully about this passage and the information you learned or read in another piece. How is this information alike in both passages? How is it different? Use details from the passages to support your comparison.

Write, write, write, explain, explain, explain!

Name _____   **Comprehension: Informational**

Compare information from this passage to information from another passage.

Vocabulary Box

compare	
information	
passage	

Student-Friendly Translation

Tell what is the same and what is different about the facts from this article and another you have read. Use details from the passage to explain your ideas.

This means:

Think carefully about this passage and the information you learned or read in another piece. How is this information alike in both passages? How is it different? Use details from the passages to support your comparison.

Write, write, write, explain, explain, explain!

Comprehension
of Functional Texts

11

Name _____   **Comprehension: Functional**

Identify the main idea of this selection.

Vocabulary Box

identify	explain, tell, point out, give details about
main idea	main point, topic, subject
selection	passage, article

Student-Friendly Translation

Give details about the major point of this passage. Use details from the
passage to explain your ideas.

This means:

Decide what the most important point of this passage is. Every sentence
in the passage should have something to do with that idea. Explain
what that idea is and use details from the passage to tell more about it.

Write, write, write, explain, explain, explain!

Name _____   **Comprehension: Functional**

Identify the main idea of this selection.

Vocabulary Box

identify	
main idea	
selection	

Student-Friendly Translation

Give details about the major point of this passage. Use details from the passage to explain your ideas.

This means:

Decide what the most important point of this passage is. Every sentence in the passage should have something to do with that idea. Explain what that idea is and use details from the passage to tell more about it.

Write, write, write, explain, explain, explain!

Name _____   **Comprehension: Functional**

Summarize what the passage explains how to do.

Vocabulary Box

summarize	tell the main points, explain in one sentence
passage	selection, article, piece
explains how to do	involves, expects

Student-Friendly Translation

> Tell the main points of the assignment the passage is explaining how to do. Use details from the selection to explain your ideas.

This means:

> What is the job being described in the passage? What does it explain how to do? Tell the main points in one sentence. If the job was to clean your desk, what points would you have to include? You might have to take everything out of your desk, remove rubbish or dirt, organize your things, and put them back into your desk. What steps are included in the task described in the passage? Use details from the passage to explain your ideas.

Write, write, write, explain, explain, explain!

Name _____   **Comprehension: Functional**

Summarize what the passage explains how to do.

Vocabulary Box

summarize	
passage	
explains how to do	

Student-Friendly Translation

> Tell the main points of the assignment the passage is explaining how to do. Use details from the selection to explain your ideas.

This means:

> What is the job being described in the passage? What does it explain how to do? Tell the main points in one sentence. If the job was to clean your desk, what points would you have to include? You might have to take everything out of your desk, remove rubbish or dirt, organize your things, and put them back into your desk. What steps are included in the task described in the passage? Use details from the passage to explain your ideas.

Write, write, write, explain, explain, explain!

Name _____   **Comprehension: Functional**

Estimate how much time it would take to follow the instructions.

Vocabulary Box

estimate	make an informed guess, calculate approximately
how much time	how many minutes, hours, days, or years
to follow the instructions	to do the job described in the passage, to finish the assignment

Student-Friendly Translation

> Make a careful guess about the amount of time it would take to finish the job described in the passage. Use details from the passage to explain why it would take that amount of time.

This means:

> How much time would it take someone to do the job described in the passage? Imagine that each step is pretty easy, but plan how long each part would take and then add the times together. Be sure to tell why you think it would take that amount of time using details from the passage.

Write, write, write, explain, explain, explain!

Name _____　　　**Comprehension: Functional**

Estimate how much time it would take to follow the instructions.

Vocabulary Box

estimate	
how much time	
to follow the instructions	

Student-Friendly Translation

> Make a careful guess about the amount of time it would take to finish the job described in the passage. Use details from the passage to explain why it would take that amount of time.

This means:

> How much time would it take someone to do the job described in the passage? Imagine that each step is pretty easy, but plan how long each part would take and then add the times together. Be sure to tell why you think it would take that amount of time using details from the passage.

Write, write, write, explain, explain, explain!

Name _____   **Comprehension: Functional**

Identify who would need this information and how they would use it.

Vocabulary Box

identify	point out, name, describe
need this information	use the directions, perform the task
how they would use it	what would they do with these directions

Student-Friendly Translation

> Describe who would need to perform the task described in the passage. Why would they need to follow these directions? How would they use this information? Explain by using details in the passage.

This means:

> Think about what kind of person would use this information. It doesn't have to be someone you know. How would someone use this information? Use details from the passage to explain why you have these ideas.

Write, write, write, explain, explain, explain!

Name _____   **Comprehension: Functional**

Identify who would need this information and how they would use it.

Vocabulary Box

identify	
need this information	
how they would use it	

Student-Friendly Translation

> Describe who would need to perform the task described in the passage. Why would they need to follow these directions? How would they use this information? Explain by using details in the passage.

This means:

> Think about what kind of person would use this information. It doesn't have to be someone you know. How would someone use this information? Use details from the passage to explain why you have these ideas.

Write, write, write, explain, explain, explain!

SECTION 3

Application

(Organization, Clarification, Conclusions)

Application of Narrative Texts 12

Name _____   **Application: Narrative**

Tell the steps a character takes to solve a problem.

Vocabulary Box

steps	things someone does, procedures, list in order
character	a person or animal in the story
solve a problem	figure out what to do, fix a difficulty or setback

Student-Friendly Translation

> Explain the things a person or animal does to fix a setback in the story. Give details from the passage that help explain!

This means:

> Every story has at least one problem. Think of a problem or difficulty in this story. What does the main character do to fix the problem? Sometimes the problems aren't exactly bad things. Sometimes the problem is a challenge that the characters need to rise to. But problems are the main events in the story. Tell what the characters do to get through the problems. Use details from the story to explain.

Write, write, write, explain, explain, explain!

Name _____   **Application: Narrative**

Tell the steps a character takes to solve a problem.

Vocabulary Box

steps	
character	
solve a problem	

Student-Friendly Translation

> Explain the things a person or animal does to fix a setback in the story. Give details from the passage that help explain!

This means:

> Every story has at least one problem. Think of a problem or difficulty in this story. What does the main character do to fix the problem? Sometimes the problems aren't exactly bad things. Sometimes the problem is a challenge that the characters need to rise to. But problems are the main events in the story. Tell what the characters do to get through the problems. Use details from the story to explain.

Write, write, write, explain, explain, explain!

Name _____   **Application: Narrative**

Tell how your prior knowledge helped you understand the story.

Vocabulary Box

prior knowledge	what you knew before you read this passage, what you know from your life
helped you understand	made it easier when you were reading this passage
the story	the passage, piece, book, selection

Student-Friendly Translation

> What did you know before you read this passage that made it easier for you to understand this selection? Give details from the passage that help explain!

This means:

> Think about what you know about this subject. Maybe you know a lot, or maybe you think you know nothing. Was the vocabulary familiar? Was the main idea something you had thought about before? Were the characters like people you know? You must think of something you already knew that helped you. Use details from the story to explain.

Write, write, write, explain, explain, explain!

Name _____　　　　**Application: Narrative**

Tell how your prior knowledge helped you understand the story.

Vocabulary Box

prior knowledge	
helped you understand	
the story	

Student-Friendly Translation

> What did you know before you read this passage that made it easier for you to understand this selection? Give details from the passage that help explain!

This means:

> Think about what you know about this subject. Maybe you know a lot, or maybe you think you know nothing. Was the vocabulary familiar? Was the main idea something you had thought about before? Were the characters like people you know? You must think of something you already knew that helped you. Use details from the story to explain.

Write, write, write, explain, explain, explain!

Name _____   **Application: Narrative**

Describe how the mood changed during the story.

Vocabulary Box

describe how	explain, give details
mood	feeling of the story, main emotion
changed	grew, improved, got worse, learned
during the story	from the beginning to the end, from the start to the finish

Student-Friendly Translation

Explain how the feeling in the story changed during the story. Use details from the story to explain your ideas.

This means:

Think about the main feeling in the story. Is the main character mostly happy, sad, angry, or hurt? How does that mood or feeling change during the story? What happens that makes the mood change? Use details from the story to explain your ideas.

Write, write, write, explain, explain, explain!

Name _____   **Application: Narrative**

Describe how the mood changed during the story.

Vocabulary Box

describe how	
mood	
changed	
during the story	

Student-Friendly Translation

> Explain how the feeling in the story changed during the story. Use
> details from the story to explain your ideas.

This means:

> Think about the main feeling in the story. Is the main character mostly
> happy, sad, angry, or hurt? How does that mood or feeling change
> during the story? What happens that makes the mood change? Use
> details from the story to explain your ideas.

Write, write, write, explain, explain, explain!

Name _____   **Application: Narrative**

Tell how the main character changed during the story.

Vocabulary Box

tell how	explain, give details
main character	most important person or animal
changed	grew, improved, got worse, learned
during the story	from the beginning to the end, from the start to the finish

Student-Friendly Translation

Explain how the person or animal in the story changed during the story.

This means:

All stories have characters and all characters change during the story. Using details from the story, explain what changes you see in the character. Usually the character learns something important or changes his or her thinking in some way. Use details from the story to explain your ideas.

Write, write, write, explain, explain, explain!

Name _____   **Application: Narrative**

Tell how the main character changed during the story.

Vocabulary Box

tell how	
main character	
changed	
during the story	

Student-Friendly Translation

Explain how the person or animal in the story changed during the story.

This means:

All stories have characters and all characters change during the story. Using details from the story, explain what changes you see in the character. Usually the character learns something important or changes his or her thinking in some way. Use details from the story to explain your ideas.

Write, write, write, explain, explain, explain!

Name _____   **Application: Narrative**

Tell about the plot development in the story.

Vocabulary Box

plot	the events that happen in the story, problem
development	changes, progress
the story	the passage, piece, book, selection

Student-Friendly Translation

> Describe the events and problems in the story. Give details from the passage that help explain!

This means:

> Think about what happens in the story. Describe the major events or problems from the story. Use details from the story to explain.

Write, write, write, explain, explain, explain!

Name _____   **Application: Narrative**

Tell about the plot development in the story.

Vocabulary Box

plot	
development	
the story	

Student-Friendly Translation

Describe the events and problems in the story. Give details from the passage that help explain!

This means:

Think about what happens in the story. Describe the major events or problems from the story. Use details from the story to explain.

Write, write, write, explain, explain, explain!

Name _____   **Application: Narrative**

Why do you think the author wrote this passage?

Vocabulary Box

author	the person who wrote this piece
passage	piece, selection, story

Student-Friendly Translation

> Why do you think the person who wrote this piece, wrote it? Give details from the passage that help explain!

This means:

> Why would someone write this story? Did he or she want to teach you something or just entertain you? Do you think this story or something like it could have happened to him or her? "He or she wrote it to make money" is not a good answer! Why did the author choose this story? Use details from the story to explain.

Write, write, write, explain, explain, explain!

Name _____   **Application: Narrative**

Why do you think the author wrote this passage?

Vocabulary Box

author	
passage	

Student-Friendly Translation

Why do you think the person who wrote this piece, wrote it? Give details from the passage that help explain!

This means:

Why would someone write this story? Did he or she want to teach you something or just entertain you? Do you think this story or something like it could have happened to him or her? "He or she wrote it to make money" is not a good answer! Why did the author choose this story? Use details from the story to explain.

Write, write, write, explain, explain, explain!

Application of Informational Texts 13

Name _____   **Application: Informational**

Describe the organizational structure used in this article.

Vocabulary Box

describe	tell about, explain with details
organizational structure	how the article is arranged (usual choices: cause-effect, compare-contrast, problem-solution, main idea-detail)
article	informational writing, sometimes found in a magazine

Student-Friendly Translation

Explain with details how the passage is arranged. Use details from the story to explain your ideas.

This means:

Does the article show what happens because of other things happening (cause-effect)? Does it compare two or more things (compare-contrast)? Does the article present a problem and a way to solve it (problem-solution)? Is there a main idea and details that tell more about it (main idea-details)? Use details from the story to explain your ideas.

Write, write, write, explain, explain, explain!

Name _____   **Application: Informational**

Describe the organizational structure used in this article.

Vocabulary Box

describe	
organizational structure	
article	

Student-Friendly Translation

> Explain with details how the passage is arranged. Use details from the story to explain your ideas.

This means:

> Does the article show what happens because of other things happening (cause-effect)? Does it compare two or more things (compare-contrast)? Does the article present a problem and a way to solve it (problem-solution)? Is there a main idea and details that tell more about it (main idea-details)? Use details from the story to explain your ideas.

Write, write, write, explain, explain, explain!

Name _____   **Application: Informational**

Tell what clue words you used to decide which organizational structure was used.

Vocabulary Box

clue words	hints, ideas, signs, words that give you clues
decide	figure out, determine, conclude
organizational structure	how the article is arranged (usual choices: cause-effect, compare-contrast, problem-solution, main idea-detail)

Student-Friendly Translation

How is the passage arranged? What signal words help you figure it out? Use details from the story to explain your ideas.

This means:

Does the article show what happens because of other things happening (cause-effect)? Does it compare two or more things (compare-contrast)? Does the article present a problem and a way to solve it (problem-solution)? Is there a main idea and details that tell more about it (main idea-details)? Look for signal words and details that explain why you chose the organizational structure.

Write, write, write, explain, explain, explain!

Name _____   **Application: Informational**

Tell what clue words you used to decide which organizational structure was used.

Vocabulary Box

clue words	
decide	
organizational structure	

Student-Friendly Translation

How is the passage arranged? What signal words help you figure it out? Use details from the story to explain your ideas.

This means:

Does the article show what happens because of other things happening (cause-effect)? Does it compare two or more things (compare-contrast)? Does the article present a problem and a way to solve it (problem-solution)? Is there a main idea and details that tell more about it (main idea-details)? Look for signal words and details that explain why you chose the organizational structure.

Write, write, write, explain, explain, explain!

Name _____ **Application: Informational**

If there were no text features included in the article, could you do the task described?

Vocabulary Box

text features	drawing, figure, plan, map, chart, table
included in the article	with this passage
do the task	finish this job or assignment

Student-Friendly Translation

If there were no pictures, would you still be able to follow the instructions? Use details from the passage to explain your answer. It's okay to say that you couldn't, but you still have to explain!

This means:

Cover up the pictures and reread the directions. Can you figure out what to do? How do the pictures help you figure it out? Explain using details from the passage and from the text features.

Write, write, write, explain, explain, explain!

Name _____   **Application: Informational**

If there were no text features included in the article, could you do the task described?

Vocabulary Box

text features	
included in the article	
do the task	

Student-Friendly Translation

> If there were no pictures, would you still be able to follow the instructions? Use details from the passage to explain your answer. It's okay to say that you couldn't, but you still have to explain!

This means:

> Cover up the pictures and reread the directions. Can you figure out what to do? How do the pictures help you figure it out? Explain using details from the passage and from the text features.

Write, write, write, explain, explain, explain!

Name _____   **Application: Informational**

How is the article organized?

Vocabulary Box

how	explain, tell more about, give details
article	piece, passage, selection
organized	arranged, put together

Student-Friendly Translation

> Explain how the facts in this passage are put together. Tell why you think that, using details from the article.

This means:

> Some ways that articles are organized are the following: cause-effect, compare-contrast, problem-solution, main idea-detail. Does the article show what happens because of other things happening (cause-effect)? Does it compare two or more things (compare-contrast)? Does the article present a problem and a way to solve it (problem-solution)? Is there a main idea and details that tell more about it (main idea-details)? Use examples from the article to show what you mean.

Write, write, write, explain, explain, explain!

Name _____   **Application: Informational**

How is the article organized?

Vocabulary Box

how	
article	
organized	

Student-Friendly Translation

> Explain how the facts in this passage are put together. Tell why you think that, using details from the article.

This means:

> Some ways that articles are organized are the following: cause-effect, compare-contrast, problem-solution, main idea-detail. Does the article show what happens because of other things happening (cause-effect)? Does it compare two or more things (compare-contrast)? Does the article present a problem and a way to solve it (problem-solution)? Is there a main idea and details that tell more about it (main idea-details)? Use examples from the article to show what you mean.

Write, write, write, explain, explain, explain!

Name _____　　　　**Application: Informational**

This article is organized in sequential order. Why is this the best structure for this article?

Vocabulary Box

organized	arranged the sentences and the facts
sequential order	steps or events in time order
best	most appropriate, makes the most sense, fits best
organizational structure	way to arrange the information
article	piece, passage, selection

Student-Friendly Translation

The person who wrote the article put the steps or events in time order. Tell why this way of arranging the information makes sense. Give details from the article to support your ideas.

This means:

The article is written in time order: first, second, then, next, last. Why does this make sense for this article? Show why it works using details from the article.

Write, write, write, explain, explain, explain!

Name _____   **Application: Informational**

This article is organized in sequential order. Why is this the best structure for this article?

Vocabulary Box

organized	
sequential order	
best	
organizational structure	
article	

Student-Friendly Translation

> The person who wrote the article put the steps or events in time order. Tell why this way of arranging the information makes sense. Give details from the article to support your ideas.

This means:

> The article is written in time order: first, second, then, next, last. Why does this make sense for this article? Show why it works using details from the article.

Write, write, write, explain, explain, explain!

Name _____   **Application: Informational**

Use facts from this article to write a story.

Vocabulary Box

facts	facts, true information, accurate data
story	made-up story, fiction

Student-Friendly Translation

> Use the true information in the article to write a made-up story.

This means:

> Write a story with characters, setting, problem, and solution using some of the facts found in this article. Be sure to include at least three facts from the article in your story. Be creative!

Write, write, write, explain, explain, explain!

Name _____   **Application: Informational**

Use facts from this article to write a story.

Vocabulary Box

facts	
story	

Student-Friendly Translation

Use the true information in the article to write a made-up story.

This means:

Write a story with characters, setting, problem, and solution using some of the facts found in this article. Be sure to include at least three facts from the article in your story. Be creative!

Write, write, write, explain, explain, explain!

Application of Functional Texts 14

Name _____ **Application: Functional**

What added information would you need to do this task?

Vocabulary Box

added information	other instructions, more details
this task	this assignment, job

Student-Friendly Translation

> Point out what other instructions could help you finish this assignment. Use details from the passage to explain your ideas.

This means:

> Read carefully through the instructions. What else would help you do the job? Sometimes it takes a lot of thought to imagine other details you would like to have. Look at each step. What parts are confusing or could be explained in more detail? Remember, you need to find some details to add in. Explain why these details are necessary by using the information given to you.

Write, write, write, explain, explain, explain!

Name _____   **Application: Functional**

What added information would you need to do this task?

Vocabulary Box

added information	
this task	

Student-Friendly Translation

> Point out what other instructions could help you finish this assignment. Use details from the passage to explain your ideas.

This means:

> Read carefully through the instructions. What else would help you do the job? Sometimes it takes a lot of thought to imagine other details you would like to have. Look at each step. What parts are confusing or could be explained in more detail? Remember, you need to find some details to add in. Explain why these details are necessary by using the information given to you.

Write, write, write, explain, explain, explain!

SECTION 4

Analysis

(Compare Content to Personal Experiences)

Analysis of Narrative Texts 15

Name _____   **Analysis: Narrative**

How are the events in the story like things that have happened to you?

Vocabulary Box

events	something that happened in the story
like	similar, compared to

Student-Friendly Translation

Tell about a time when something happened to you that is at all like the things that happen in the story. Use details from the story to explain your ideas.

This means:

Think about the main things that happen in the story. Think about things you've done that are like those events. Remember, you are looking for things you know about that are like the actions in the story. You must think of something that is like the events of the story. Use details from the story to explain your ideas.

Write, write, write, explain, explain, explain!

Name _____   **Analysis: Narrative**

How are the events in the story like things that have happened to you?

Vocabulary Box

events	
like	

Student-Friendly Translation

Tell about a time when something happened to you that is at all like the things that happen in the story. Use details from the story to explain your ideas.

This means:

Think about the main things that happen in the story. Think about things you've done that are like those events. Remember, you are looking for things you know about that are like the actions in the story. You must think of something that is like the events of the story. Use details from the story to explain your ideas.

Write, write, write, explain, explain, explain!

Name _____   **Analysis: Narrative**

Compare the characters in the story with someone you know.

Vocabulary Box

compare	tell how they are the same or different
characters	people or animals in the story
story	book, passage, selection
someone you know	a person you are familiar with

Student-Friendly Translation

> Tell what is the same and different about the characters in the story and a person you know.

This means:

> Think of the main person in the story. Is there anything that is like someone you know? If not, it is okay to make something up. The idea is to answer the question telling similarities and differences with the story. If you can do that, it doesn't matter if you have to make up a person. Use details from the story to explain your ideas.

Write, write, write, explain, explain, explain!

Name _____   **Analysis: Narrative**

Compare the characters in the story with someone you know.

Vocabulary Box

compare	
characters	
story	
someone you know	

Student-Friendly Translation

Tell what is the same and different about the characters in the story and a person you know.

This means:

Think of the main person in the story. Is there anything that is like someone you know? If not, it is okay to make something up. The idea is to answer the question telling similarities and differences with the story. If you can do that, it doesn't matter if you have to make up a person. Use details from the story to explain your ideas.

Write, write, write, explain, explain, explain!

Name _____   **Analysis: Narrative**

How are your feelings similar to or different from the main character's feelings?

Vocabulary Box

your feelings	how you feel, your emotions, your thoughts
similar or different	compare and contrast, same or different
character's feelings	emotions, thoughts of the main person (or animal) in the story

Student-Friendly Translation

> Give details about how your emotions and thoughts are the same as or different from the emotions and thoughts of the main person (or animal) in the story.

This means:

> Think about how the main character in the story feels. His or her feelings may change during the story, but think about his or her feelings at one part of the story. Have you ever felt that way? Try to relate the main character's feelings to yours. Give lots of details about how your feelings and the main character's feelings are alike. Tell why the main character feels that way, using details from the story. Tell why you felt that way, giving details from your life.

Write, write, write, explain, explain, explain!

Name _____   **Analysis: Narrative**

How are your feelings similar to or different from the main character's feelings?

Vocabulary Box

your feelings	
similar or different	
character's feelings	

Student-Friendly Translation

Give details about how your emotions and thoughts are the same as or different from the emotions and thoughts of the main person (or animal) in the story.

This means:

Think about how the main character in the story feels. His or her feelings may change during the story, but think about his or her feelings at one part of the story. Have you ever felt that way? Try to relate the main character's feelings to yours. Give lots of details about how your feelings and the main character's feelings are alike. Tell why the main character feels that way, using details from the story. Tell why you felt that way, giving details from your life.

Write, write, write, explain, explain, explain!

Name _____   **Analysis: Narrative**

Explain whether you would act the same as the main character.

Vocabulary Box

explain	tell why, give details from the story
main character	most important person or animal from the story

Student-Friendly Translation

Think of the main character. Explain, using story details for support, whether you would act the same way he or she did.

This means:

Give details about whether you would do the same as the main character did in the story or whether you would do something different. Remember to use details from the story to explain your ideas.

Write, write, write, explain, explain, explain!

Name _____   **Analysis: Narrative**

Explain whether you would act the same as the main character.

Vocabulary Box

explain	
main character	

Student-Friendly Translation

> Think of the main character. Explain, using story details for support, whether you would act the same way he or she did.

This means:

> Give details about whether you would do the same as the main character did in the story or whether you would do something different. Remember to use details from the story to explain your ideas.

Write, write, write, explain, explain, explain!

Name _____   **Analysis: Narrative**

Which part interested you most?

Vocabulary Box

which part	tell what details from the story
interested	attracted you, excited you, fascinated you

Student-Friendly Translation

Tell exactly what parts about the characters, action, plot, or setting excited you the most. Give details from the story to explain!

This means:

Find a part of the story that fascinated or interested you. Think about what details the author used that caught your interest. Explain those details and why they were interesting to you. Remember, the question asks what part interested you most. If you don't talk about a part that excited you, you are not answering the question correctly. Find something interesting and give details!

Write, write, write, explain, explain, explain!

Name _____   **Analysis: Narrative**

Which part interested you most?

Vocabulary Box

which part	
interested	

Student-Friendly Translation

> Tell exactly what parts about the characters, action, plot, or setting excited you the most. Give details from the story to explain!

This means:

> Find a part of the story that fascinated or interested you. Think about what details the author used that caught your interest. Explain those details and why they were interesting to you. Remember, the question asks what part interested you most. If you don't talk about a part that excited you, you are not answering the question correctly. Find something interesting and give details!

Write, write, write, explain, explain, explain!

Name _____   **Analysis: Narrative**

How does the setting compare with where you live?

Vocabulary Box

setting	place where the story happens, set, site, location (remember: setting also includes time period or year)
compare	tell how they are the same or different

Student-Friendly Translation

Tell what is the same and different about the place or the time period in the story and a place or time you know about. Include details from the story.

This means:

Think of all of the places and times in the story. Is there anything that is like somewhere you have been? If not, it is okay to make something up. The idea is to answer the question telling similarities and differences with the setting in the story. If you can do that, it doesn't matter if you have to make up a place. Be sure to include details from the story.

Write, write, write, explain, explain, explain!

Name _____   **Analysis: Narrative**

How does the setting compare with where you live?

Vocabulary Box

setting	
compare	

Student-Friendly Translation

> Tell what is the same and different about the place or the time period in the story and a place or time you know about. Include details from the story.

This means:

> Think of all of the places and times in the story. Is there anything that is like somewhere you have been? If not, it is okay to make something up. The idea is to answer the question telling similarities and differences with the setting in the story. If you can do that, it doesn't matter if you have to make up a place. Be sure to include details from the story.

Write, write, write, explain, explain, explain!

Name _____   **Analysis: Narrative**

Tell about a time when you experienced an incident like the one in the story.

Vocabulary Box

experienced	lived through, did something
incident	plot, things that happened, action, event
story	book, passage, selection, text

Student-Friendly Translation

Tell what is the same and different between things that have happened to you and things that happened to the characters in the story.

This means:

Think of all of the actions and events in the story. Is there anything that is like something that has happened to you? If not, it is okay to make something up. The idea is to answer the question telling similarities and differences with the story. If you can do that, it doesn't matter if you have to make up some actions. Be sure to include details from the story.

Write, write, write, explain, explain, explain!

Name _____   **Analysis: Narrative**

Tell about a time when you experienced an incident like the one in the story.

Vocabulary Box

experienced	
incident	
story	

Student-Friendly Translation

> Tell what is the same and different between things that have happened to you and things that happened to the characters in the story.

This means:

> Think of all of the actions and events in the story. Is there anything that is like something that has happened to you? If not, it is okay to make something up. The idea is to answer the question telling similarities and differences with the story. If you can do that, it doesn't matter if you have to make up some actions. Be sure to include details from the story.

Write, write, write, explain, explain, explain!

Name _____   **Analysis: Narrative**

Explain how the author's message connects to your own life.

Vocabulary Box

explain	decide how, judge, tell, describe
author's message	what the author wanted you to learn, the moral of the story
connects to your own life	relates to your life, makes sense in your own life, could be useful for your own life

Student-Friendly Translation

Decide and describe how the moral of the story could be useful in your own life. Give details from the story and from your life to explain.

This means:

Think about the moral of the story. What is the story about and what did you learn from it? How does that message connect to your life? What lesson from the story could you use in your life? Remember, it is okay to make something up if you need to! Give details from the story to support your ideas.

Write, write, write, explain, explain, explain!

Name _____ **Analysis: Narrative**

Explain how the author's message connects to your own life.

Vocabulary Box

explain	
author's message	
connects to your own life	

Student-Friendly Translation

> Decide and describe how the moral of the story could be useful in your own life. Give details from the story and from your life to explain.

This means:

> Think about the moral of the story. What is the story about and what did you learn from it? How does that message connect to your life? What lesson from the story could you use in your life? Remember, it is okay to make something up if you need to! Give details from the story to support your ideas.

Write, write, write, explain, explain, explain!

Name _____   **Analysis: Narrative**

Make a list of questions you would like to ask the author.

Vocabulary Box

author	person who wrote the story

Student-Friendly Translation

> What would you like to ask the person who wrote the story? Be sure to include details from the story to explain why you want to ask those questions.

This means:

> Think about the story. If you could talk to the person who wrote it, what would you like to know about the story? Think about the parts of the story, the characters, the setting, the plot, the problem, and the solution. What more would you like to know? Ask specific questions using the details from the story. Avoid questions about the author's personal life. Focus on the story.

Write, write, write, explain, explain, explain!

Name _____   **Analysis: Narrative**

Make a list of questions you would like to ask the author.

Vocabulary Box

author	

Student-Friendly Translation

> What would you like to ask the person who wrote the story? Be sure to include details from the story to explain why you want to ask those questions.

This means:

> Think about the story. If you could talk to the person who wrote it, what would you like to know about the story? Think about the parts of the story, the characters, the setting, the plot, the problem, and the solution. What more would you like to know? Ask specific questions using the details from the story. Avoid questions about the author's personal life. Focus on the story.

Write, write, write, explain, explain, explain!

Name _____   **Analysis: Narrative**

What questions would you like to ask the main character?

Vocabulary Box

main character	the main person or animal in the story

Student-Friendly Translation

What would you like to ask the main person or animal in the story? Be sure to include details from the story.

This means:

Think about the parts of the story, the characters, the setting, the plot, the problem, and the solution. What more would you like to know? Think of questions for the people or animals in the story. Imagine you could sit down and talk to them as real people. What more would you like to know about what they did or said in the story? Ask specific questions using the details from the story. Focus on the story.

Write, write, write, explain, explain, explain!

Name _____   **Analysis: Narrative**

What questions would you like to ask the main character?

Vocabulary Box

main character	

Student-Friendly Translation

What would you like to ask the main person or animal in the story? Be sure to include details from the story.

This means:

Think about the parts of the story, the characters, the setting, the plot, the problem, and the solution. What more would you like to know? Think of questions for the people or animals in the story. Imagine you could sit down and talk to them as real people. What more would you like to know about what they did or said in the story? Ask specific questions using the details from the story. Focus on the story.

Write, write, write, explain, explain, explain!

Name _____ **Analysis: Narrative**

What are the attitudes of the main character?

Vocabulary Box

attitudes	outlook, thoughts, way of thinking
main character	the most important person or animal in the passage

Student-Friendly Translation

What are the thoughts or intentions of the person or animal in the passage? Use details from the passage to explain your ideas.

This means:

What can you figure out about the main character that isn't exactly explained to you in the passage? By what the character says, does, or thinks, imagine what kind of person he or she is and why he or she does things. Explain your thinking!

Write, write, write, explain, explain, explain!

Name _____   **Analysis: Narrative**

What are the attitudes of the main character?

Vocabulary Box

attitudes	
main character	

Student-Friendly Translation

> What are the thoughts or intentions of the person or animal in the passage? Use details from the passage to explain your ideas.

This means:

> What can you figure out about the main character that isn't exactly explained to you in the passage? By what the character says, does, or thinks, imagine what kind of person he or she is and why he or she does things. Explain your thinking!

Write, write, write, explain, explain, explain!

Name _____   **Analysis: Narrative**

What are the feelings of the main character?

Vocabulary Box

feelings	emotions, outlook
main character	the most important person or animal in the passage

Student-Friendly Translation

Figure out the emotions or outlook of the most important person or animal in the passage. Use details from the passage to explain your ideas.

This means:

What can you figure out about the main character that isn't exactly explained to you in the passage? By what the character says, does, or thinks, imagine what kind of person he or she is and how he or she feels. Explain your thinking!

Write, write, write, explain, explain, explain!

Name _____   **Analysis: Narrative**

What are the feelings of the main character?

Vocabulary Box

feelings	
main character	

Student-Friendly Translation

Figure out the emotions or outlook of the most important person or animal in the passage. Use details from the passage to explain your ideas.

This means:

What can you figure out about the main character that isn't exactly explained to you in the passage? By what the character says, does, or thinks, imagine what kind of person he or she is and how he or she feels. Explain your thinking!

Write, write, write, explain, explain, explain!

Name _____   **Analysis: Narrative**

What are the motives of the main character?

Vocabulary Box

motives	reasons for doing things, intention, drive
main character	the most important person or animal in the passage

Student-Friendly Translation

Figure out reasons why the person or animal in the passage does what he or she does. Use details from the passage to explain your ideas.

This means:

What can you figure out about the main character that isn't explained to you in the passage? By what the character says, does, or thinks, imagine what kind of person he or she is and why he or she does things. Explain your thinking!

Write, write, write, explain, explain, explain!

Name _____   **Analysis: Narrative**

What are the motives of the main character?

Vocabulary Box

motives	
main character	

Student-Friendly Translation

Figure out reasons why the person or animal in the passage does what he or she does. Use details from the passage to explain your ideas.

This means:

What can you figure out about the main character that isn't explained to you in the passage? By what the character says, does, or thinks, imagine what kind of person he or she is and why he or she does things. Explain your thinking!

Write, write, write, explain, explain, explain!

Analysis of Informational Texts 16

Name _____   **Analysis: Informational**

What added information would you like to read about?

Vocabulary Box

what added information	what other facts, what else

Student-Friendly Translation

Think of other facts you would like to read about. Be sure to use examples from this passage to explain what you would like to read about.

This means:

What else does this article make you think of? What could possibly help you? What other subject would you like to read about that is related to this one? Remember to use details from the article.

Write, write, write, explain, explain, explain!

Name _____   **Analysis: Informational**

What added information would you like to read about?

Vocabulary Box

what added information	

Student-Friendly Translation

Think of other facts you would like to read about. Be sure to use examples from this passage to explain what you would like to read about.

This means:

What else does this article make you think of? What could possibly help you? What other subject would you like to read about that is related to this one? Remember to use details from the article.

Write, write, write, explain, explain, explain!

Name _____   **Analysis: Informational**

Point out facts in the text that you didn't know before.

Vocabulary Box

point out	identify, find, show
facts	information, data
text	passage, piece, selection, writing

Student-Friendly Translation

Point out facts in the passage that you didn't know before. Give plenty of facts from the article and include details about you.

This means:

Find facts in the piece that are new to you. Explain that they are new to you, using your own words to describe the details about them. Remember to include the details from the story to explain.

Write, write, write, explain, explain, explain!

Name _____   **Analysis: Informational**

Point out facts in the text that you didn't know before.

Vocabulary Box

point out	
facts	
text	

Student-Friendly Translation

Point out facts in the passage that you didn't know before. Give plenty of facts from the article and include details about you.

This means:

Find facts in the piece that are new to you. Explain that they are new to you, using your own words to describe the details about them. Remember to include the details from the story to explain.

Write, write, write, explain, explain, explain!

Name _____   **Analysis: Informational**

Based on your prior knowledge, explain whether the facts in the selection go along with what you already knew or not.

Vocabulary Box

prior knowledge	what you already know, knowledge you already have about the topic
explain	tell how, give details
facts	knowledge, information
selection	passage, book, story, text
go along with what you already knew or not	match or don't match, agree or differ

Student-Friendly Translation

Explain how the facts in this passage go along with or go against what you knew before about this subject.

This means:

What are the main facts from this passage? What did you know about this subject before reading this passage? Do you agree with everything you read in this passage? Use details from the passage to explain whether you agree or disagree with the information you read. It is okay to agree with the information!

Write, write, write, explain, explain, explain!

Name _____   **Analysis: Informational**

Based on your prior knowledge, explain whether the facts in the selection go along with what you already knew or not.

Vocabulary Box

prior knowledge	
explain	
facts	
selection	
go along with what you already knew or not	

Student-Friendly Translation

> Explain how the facts in this passage go along with or go against what you knew before about this subject.

This means:

> What are the main facts from this passage? What did you know about this subject before reading this passage? Do you agree with everything you read in this passage? Use details from the passage to explain whether you agree or disagree with the information you read. It is okay to agree with the information!

Write, write, write, explain, explain, explain!

Name _____   **Analysis: Informational**

Tell what course of action you might take now that you've read this selection.

Vocabulary Box

tell	describe, give details
course of action	direction, procedure, process
now that you've read this selection	since you read this passage

Student-Friendly Translation

Give details about what you would do with the knowledge you learned from this passage.

This means:

What did you learn from the passage? What will you do now that you have this knowledge? Did the passage teach you how to do something or how to change something in your life? Use details from the passage to explain what you would do.

Write, write, write, explain, explain, explain!

Name _____   **Analysis: Informational**

Tell what course of action you might take now that you've read this selection.

Vocabulary Box

tell	
course of action	
now that you've read this selection	

Student-Friendly Translation

> Give details about what you would do with the knowledge you learned from this passage.

This means:

> What did you learn from the passage? What will you do now that you have this knowledge? Did the passage teach you how to do something or how to change something in your life? Use details from the passage to explain what you would do.

Write, write, write, explain, explain, explain!

Name _____   **Analysis: Informational**

Draw a conclusion after reading this piece.

Vocabulary Box

draw a conclusion	tell what you learned, moral
after reading this piece	from reading this article, passage

Student-Friendly Translation

Tell what you learned from this piece.

This means:

Think about what you learned from this piece. Thinking about your life and your experiences, think about what you learned. Write your conclusion in one sentence and support it with details from the piece.

Write, write, write, explain, explain, explain!

Name _____   **Analysis: Informational**

Draw a conclusion after reading this piece.

Vocabulary Box

draw a conclusion	
after reading this piece	

Student-Friendly Translation

Tell what you learned from this piece.

This means:

Think about what you learned from this piece. Thinking about your life and your experiences, think about what you learned. Write your conclusion in one sentence and support it with details from the piece.

Write, write, write, explain, explain, explain!

Name _____   **Analysis: Informational**

Do you agree or disagree with the information in this passage?

Vocabulary Box

agree	think the same, go along with
disagree	don't go along with, oppose
information	knowledge, details
selection	selection, piece, reading

Student-Friendly Translation

> Explain why you think the same or don't think the same as the author about the information given in this piece.

This means:

> Consider the information that you read. Do you think it is true? Do you know anything different about this subject? It is okay to agree with the author and the information that he or she wrote about, but you must give details from the passage to explain how you agree or disagree.

Write, write, write, explain, explain, explain!

Name _____ **Analysis: Informational**

Do you agree or disagree with the information in this passage?

Vocabulary Box

agree	
disagree	
information	
selection	

Student-Friendly Translation

Explain why you think the same or don't think the same as the author about the information given in this piece.

This means:

Consider the information that you read. Do you think it is true? Do you know anything different about this subject? It is okay to agree with the author and the information that he or she wrote about, but you must give details from the passage to explain how you agree or disagree.

Write, write, write, explain, explain, explain!

Name _____   **Analysis: Informational**

Compare the author's point of view to your own.

Vocabulary Box

compare	tell what is the same or different
author's point of view	what the person who wrote the passage thinks about the topic
your own (point of view)	what you think about the topic

Student-Friendly Translation

> Tell what is the same and different about what the person who wrote the passage thinks about the topic and what you think about the topic.

This means:

> Based on what the author wrote, imagine how the author felt about the topic. Does he or she seem to like the people or subject that he or she is writing about? Does the person writing look up to them? Is he or she warning people about a problem or is he or she giving you information about a good thing? Read between the lines to see what the author thinks. Then consider whether you think the same way or not. Remember to include supporting details from the writing.

Write, write, write, explain, explain, explain!

Name _____   **Analysis: Informational**

Compare the author's point of view to your own.

Vocabulary Box

compare	
author's point of view	
your own (point of view)	

Student-Friendly Translation

Tell what is the same and different about what the person who wrote the passage thinks about the topic and what you think about the topic.

This means:

Based on what the author wrote, imagine how the author felt about the topic. Does he or she seem to like the people or subject that he or she is writing about? Does the person writing look up to them? Is he or she warning people about a problem or is he or she giving you information about a good thing? Read between the lines to see what the author thinks. Then consider whether you think the same way or not. Remember to include supporting details from the writing.

Write, write, write, explain, explain, explain!

Analysis of Functional Texts 17

Name _____   **Analysis: Functional**

Explain how this information could be useful in your life.

Vocabulary Box

explain how	tell how, give details about
this information	these facts, these directions
could be useful	would be helpful, would be handy
in your life	for you

Student-Friendly Translation

Tell how this information would be helpful to you.

This means:

Even if there is no way you would ever use this information, you need to think of how it could help you. It is okay to make something up! The idea is to answer the prompt. Think about the information or facts and how they could be useful. Be sure to use examples from the text in your explanation.

Write, write, write, explain, explain, explain!

Name _____   **Analysis: Functional**

Explain how this information could be useful in your life.

Vocabulary Box

explain how	
this information	
could be useful	
in your life	

Student-Friendly Translation

Tell how this information would be helpful to you.

This means:

Even if there is no way you would ever use this information, you need to think of how it could help you. It is okay to make something up! The idea is to answer the prompt. Think about the information or facts and how they could be useful. Be sure to use examples from the text in your explanation.

Write, write, write, explain, explain, explain!

Name _____ **Analysis: Functional**

Tell what else is needed to complete this task.

Vocabulary Box

tell	think of, identify, find, point out, single out
what else	what other facts, what information
is needed	you want, you could use
to complete	to finish, to do
this task	this job, this assignment

Student-Friendly Translation

Think of other facts you could use to finish this assignment.

This means:

What is missing from this job? What else could possibly help you? Even if you feel like everything you could possibly need is in the passage, think of more information that would be useful. You have to think of something else that could help you to finish this task.

Write, write, write, explain, explain, explain!

Name _____   **Analysis: Functional**

Tell what else is needed to complete this task.

Vocabulary Box

tell	
what else	
is needed	
to complete	
this task	

Student-Friendly Translation

Think of other facts you could use to finish this assignment.

This means:

What is missing from this job? What else could possibly help you? Even if you feel like everything you could possibly need is in the passage, think of more information that would be useful. You have to think of something else that could help you to finish this task.

Write, write, write, explain, explain, explain!

Name _____   **Analysis: Functional**

How is this task similar to another task you have done?

Vocabulary Box

this task	this job, assignment or chore
similar	same as, alike, like
to another task you have done	anything you have completed, something you have finished

Student-Friendly Translation

Explain how this assignment is like anything else you have done.

This means:

Remember, you can make something up! Think about what you have done that is like this job. How is it like something you have done before? Think of specific things that are alike between the two tasks. Explain in detail, using details from the passage and details from the task you did.

Write, write, write, explain, explain, explain!

Name _____   **Analysis: Functional**

How is this task similar to another task you have done?

Vocabulary Box

this task	
similar	
to another task you have done	

Student-Friendly Translation

> Explain how this assignment is like anything else you have done.

This means:

> Remember, you can make something up! Think about what you have done that is like this job. How is it like something you have done before? Think of specific things that are alike between the two tasks. Explain in detail, using details from the passage and details from the task you did.

Write, write, write, explain, explain, explain!

Name _____　　　　　　**Analysis: Functional**

What section of the directions was difficult for you?

Vocabulary Box

what section	choose a part, point out a place
of the directions	in the instructions, guidelines
was difficult for you	was hard, didn't make sense at first

Student-Friendly Translation

Point out a place in the instructions that didn't make sense to you and explain why. Give details from the passage.

This means:

Find a hard part in the directions. Even if you completely understood everything, find a part that someone else might not understand. Give three details from the directions showing what you mean. Be very clear.

Write, write, write, explain, explain, explain!

Name _____   **Analysis: Functional**

What section of the directions was difficult for you?

Vocabulary Box

what section	
of the directions	
was difficult for you	

Student-Friendly Translation

> Point out a place in the instructions that didn't make sense to you and explain why. Give details from the passage.

This means:

> Find a hard part in the directions. Even if you completely understood everything, find a part that someone else might not understand. Give three details from the directions showing what you mean. Be very clear.

Write, write, write, explain, explain, explain!

SECTION 5

Synthesis

(Organizing the Content in New Ways)

Synthesis of Narrative Texts 18

Name _____   **Synthesis: Narrative**

What conclusions can you draw about the characters in the story?

Vocabulary Box

conclusions can you draw	make a prediction about the end of the story, tell what the story means
characters	people or animals in the story

Student-Friendly Translation

Using the people (or animals) in the story, tell what the story means.
If the story didn't end, tell what you think would happen next.

This means:

Wrap up the story. What did it mean or how will it end? Remember to refer to the details about the characters.

Write, write, write, explain, explain, explain!

Name _____   **Synthesis: Narrative**

What conclusions can you draw about the characters in the story?

Vocabulary Box

conclusions can you draw	
characters	

Student-Friendly Translation

> Using the people (or animals) in the story, tell what the story means. If the story didn't end, tell what you think would happen next.

This means:

> Wrap up the story. What did it mean or how will it end? Remember to refer to the details about the characters.

Write, write, write, explain, explain, explain!

Name _____   **Synthesis: Narrative**

Describe the characters' relationships.

Vocabulary Box

describe	explain, tell about, give details
characters'	people or animals in the book
relationships	connections with other characters

Student-Friendly Translation

Tell about the connections among people (or animals) in the book.

This means:

Are the main characters brothers, sisters, parent/child, or friends? How do they act toward one another? Do they argue or get along? Do they like each other? How are they connected? Be sure to include details from the story!

Write, write, write, explain, explain, explain!

Name _____   **Synthesis: Narrative**

Describe the characters' relationships.

Vocabulary Box

describe	
characters'	
relationships	

Student-Friendly Translation

Tell about the connections among people (or animals) in the book.

This means:

Are the main characters brothers, sisters, parent/child, or friends? How do they act toward one another? Do they argue or get along? Do they like each other? How are they connected? Be sure to include details from the story!

Write, write, write, explain, explain, explain!

Name _____   **Synthesis: Narrative**

Write a new ending for this story.

Vocabulary Box

write	create, make up, explain
new ending	different conclusion, an original finish

Student-Friendly Translation

Think of a new way to end the story. Write it!

This means:

Try to make up an original way to finish the story. Don't just change small details, change something that will change the whole feeling of the ending. What if Little Red Riding Hood had eaten the wolf? What if she had been kidnapped and held for ransom? Be funny and new! Use details that you know about the characters to make your new ending connected to the rest of the story.

Write, write, write, explain, explain, explain!

Name _____   **Synthesis: Narrative**

Write a new ending for this story.

Vocabulary Box

write	
new ending	

Student-Friendly Translation

Think of a new way to end the story. Write it!

This means:

Try to make up an original way to finish the story. Don't just change small details, change something that will change the whole feeling of the ending. What if Little Red Riding Hood had eaten the wolf? What if she had been kidnapped and held for ransom? Be funny and new! Use details that you know about the characters to make your new ending connected to the rest of the story.

Write, write, write, explain, explain, explain!

Name _____   **Synthesis: Narrative**

Identify cause-and-effect relationships in this story.

Vocabulary Box

identify	point out, find, show
cause-and-effect relationships	parts of the story that are connected because one made the other happen

Student-Friendly Translation

Point out the parts of the story that make the other parts happen.

This means:

Think about the story. What events caused other, later things to happen? Ask yourself, why did certain things happen? Most actions involve cause and effect. For example, a boy fell off his bike because a monkey ran across the road in front of him. The cause was the monkey running across the road and the effect of that action was the boy falling off his bike. Include details from the cause-and-effect partnerships that you find.

Write, write, write, explain, explain, explain!

Name _____   **Synthesis: Narrative**

Identify cause-and-effect relationships in this story.

Vocabulary Box

identify	
cause-and-effect relationships	

Student-Friendly Translation

Point out the parts of the story that make the other parts happen.

This means:

Think about the story. What events caused other, later things to happen? Ask yourself, why did certain things happen? Most actions involve cause and effect. For example, a boy fell off his bike because a monkey ran across the road in front of him. The cause was the monkey running across the road and the effect of that action was the boy falling off his bike. Include details from the cause-and-effect partnerships that you find.

Write, write, write, explain, explain, explain!

Synthesis of Informational Texts 19

Name _____   **Synthesis: Informational**

Draw inferences about the feelings of people in the selection.

Vocabulary Box

draw inferences	figure out, imagine
feelings	thoughts, way of thinking, emotions
people in the selection	people who are in the passage or article

Student-Friendly Translation

> Figure out the thoughts and emotions of the people in this reading.

This means:

> Think about how the people in this selection are feeling. One way to figure this out is to think about their actions and what they say. If they slam a door, is it because they are angry? If they smile and say kind words, are they happy? Remember to use examples from the selection.

Write, write, write, explain, explain, explain!

Name _____   **Synthesis: Informational**

Draw inferences about the feelings of people in the selection.

Vocabulary Box

draw inferences	
feelings	
people in the selection	

Student-Friendly Translation

Figure out the thoughts and emotions of the people in this reading.

This means:

Think about how the people in this selection are feeling. One way to figure this out is to think about their actions and what they say. If they slam a door, is it because they are angry? If they smile and say kind words, are they happy? Remember to use examples from the selection.

Write, write, write, explain, explain, explain!

Name _____   **Synthesis: Informational**

What can you infer about the author based on the information in the text?

Vocabulary Box

infer	figure out, imagine, conclude, assume
author	person who wrote this piece
based on the information	from the facts
text	article, passage, selection

Student-Friendly Translation

> Make a conclusion about the person who wrote this piece from the facts in this piece.

This means:

> From the passage, what can you figure out about the person who wrote it? Is he or she an expert on this information? Is there any information about the author given? Why would someone write this passage? What can you assume about the author? Remember to give three examples from the passage to support your ideas.

Write, write, write, explain, explain, explain!

Name _____   **Synthesis: Informational**

What can you infer about the author based on the information in the text?

Vocabulary Box

infer	
author	
based on the information	
text	

Student-Friendly Translation

> Make a conclusion about the person who wrote this piece from the facts in this piece.

This means:

> From the passage, what can you figure out about the person who wrote it? Is he or she an expert on this information? Is there any information about the author given? Why would someone write this passage? What can you assume about the author? Remember to give three examples from the passage to support your ideas.

Write, write, write, explain, explain, explain!

Synthesis of Functional Texts 20

Name _____   **Synthesis: Functional**

Point out what the instructions require you to do that has to be inferred.

Vocabulary Box

point out	identify, show, tell about
instructions	directions, what is necessary, what needs to be done
require you to do	show you how to do, inform you about
inferred	is expected, is suggested, is assumed

Student-Friendly Translation

Tell what needs to be done that isn't explained by the directions.

This means:

Think about each step in the directions. Is there anything that someone might not understand? Are there any parts where the directions expect you to follow through, but you haven't been directly told to? Find the requirements in the instructions that are not clearly given. Remember to include three examples.

Write, write, write, explain, explain, explain!

Name _____   **Synthesis: Functional**

Point out what the instructions require you to do that has to be inferred.

Vocabulary Box

point out	
instructions	
require you to do	
inferred	

Student-Friendly Translation

Tell what needs to be done that isn't explained by the directions.

This means:

Think about each step in the directions. Is there anything that someone might not understand? Are there any parts where the directions expect you to follow through, but you haven't been directly told to? Find the requirements in the instructions that are not clearly given. Remember to include three examples.

Write, write, write, explain, explain, explain!

SECTION 6

Evaluation

(Making a Judgment)

Evaluation of Narrative Texts **21**

Name _____   **Evaluation: Narrative**

What part of the story best shows the author's message?

Vocabulary Box

part	section
shows	tells about, expresses
author	the person who wrote this text
message	main theme, moral of the story, what the characters or you learned from reading the story

Student-Friendly Translation

> Tell what the person writing this story wanted you to learn or what the characters in this story learned. Use parts of the story to show what you think.

This means:

> What is the moral of the story? What did the characters learn or think or feel? Use parts or pieces of the story to show what you mean.

Write, write, write, explain, explain, explain!

Name _____   **Evaluation: Narrative**

What part of the story best shows the author's message?

Vocabulary Box

part	
shows	
author	
message	

Student-Friendly Translation

> Tell what the person writing this story wanted you to learn or what the characters in this story learned. Use parts of the story to show what you think.

This means:

> What is the moral of the story? What did the characters learn or think or feel? Use parts or pieces of the story to show what you mean.

Write, write, write, explain, explain, explain!

Name _____ **Analysis: Narrative**

How does the author imply the character's attitudes?

Vocabulary Box

author	person who wrote the story
imply	suggest, give details about
character	the person or animal in the passage
attitudes	outlook, thoughts, way of thinking

Student-Friendly Translation

Figure out the thoughts or intentions of the person or animal in the passage. What does the author do to give you hints about the character's thoughts? Use details from the passage to explain your ideas.

This means:

What can you figure out about the main character that isn't explained to you in the passage? By what the character says, does, or thinks, imagine what kind of person he or she is and why he or she does things. Explain your thinking!

Write, write, write, explain, explain, explain!

Name _____   **Analysis: Narrative**

How does the author imply the character's attitudes?

Vocabulary Box

author	
imply	
character	
attitudes	

Student-Friendly Translation

> Figure out the thoughts or intentions of the person or animal in the passage. What does the author do to give you hints about the character's thoughts? Use details from the passage to explain your ideas.

This means:

> What can you figure out about the main character that isn't explained to you in the passage? By what the character says, does, or thinks, imagine what kind of person he or she is and why he or she does things. Explain your thinking!

Write, write, write, explain, explain, explain!

Name _____   **Evaluation: Narrative**

Decide whether the problem and solution are realistic.

Vocabulary Box

decide	choose whether you agree or disagree, determine
problem	challenge, difficulty in the story
solution	how the difficulty is solved
realistic	like real life, it could happen

Student-Friendly Translation

> Tell whether you agree or disagree that what happens in the story could really happen in life.

This means:

> Does the story seem like something that could happen in real life? Even if no one flies, or talks to animals, does the story really seem like it would happen in the way that it does? Remember to give details from the story to support your ideas!

Write, write, write, explain, explain, explain!

Name _____   **Evaluation: Narrative**

Decide whether the problem and solution are realistic.

Vocabulary Box

decide	
problem	
solution	
realistic	

Student-Friendly Translation

> Tell whether you agree or disagree that what happens in the story could really happen in life.

This means:

> Does the story seem like something that could happen in real life? Even if no one flies, or talks to animals, does the story really seem like it would happen in the way that it does? Remember to give details from the story to support your ideas!

Write, write, write, explain, explain, explain!

Name _____   **Evaluation: Narrative**

Is the title a good one? Does it represent the passage well?

Vocabulary Box

title	name of the book or story
good	true, right, accurate
represent	stand for, signify
passage	story, selection

Student-Friendly Translation

> Tell whether you agree or disagree that the name of the book makes a good picture in your mind of the story. Use details from the story and your own life to tell why or why not.

This means:

> Does the title make sense? Before you read the book, would the title have been useful to predict what the story is about? Would you name the book the same thing? Use details from the passage to explain.

Write, write, write, explain, explain, explain!

Name _____   **Evaluation: Narrative**

Is the title a good one? Does it represent the passage well?

Vocabulary Box

title	
good	
represent	
passage	

Student-Friendly Translation

Tell whether you agree or disagree that the name of the book makes a good picture in your mind of the story. Use details from the story and your own life to tell why or why not.

This means:

Does the title make sense? Before you read the book, would the title have been useful to predict what the story is about? Would you name the book the same thing? Use details from the passage to explain.

Write, write, write, explain, explain, explain!

Name _____   **Evaluation: Narrative**

How did your feelings about the main character change during the story?

Vocabulary Box

feelings	your own ideas, what you think, opinions
main character	the main person in the story
change	grow, transform, modify
during the story	from the beginning to the end of the story

Student-Friendly Translation

How do your ideas about the character change from the beginning to the end of the story?

This means:

When you start reading, stop and think, what kind of person is this character? Read or listen carefully and think about how the character is changing during the story. What is different about your opinion of the person by the end of the story? Use details from the story to support your answer.

Write, write, write, explain, explain, explain!

Name _____   **Evaluation: Narrative**

How did your feelings about the main character change during the story?

Vocabulary Box

feelings	
main character	
change	
during the story	

Student-Friendly Translation

> How do your ideas about the character change from the beginning to the end of the story?

This means:

> When you start reading, stop and think, what kind of person is this character? Read or listen carefully and think about how the character is changing during the story. What is different about your opinion of the person by the end of the story? Use details from the story to support your answer.

Write, write, write, explain, explain, explain!

Name _____   **Evaluation: Narrative**

How did the author make you want to keep reading?

Vocabulary Box

how	explain, describe, show
author	the person who wrote the passage or story
make you want to keep reading	encouraged you to read more

Student-Friendly Translation

> Explain how the author wrote the story to keep you reading. Tell how he or she wrote suspense, action, or surprise into the story.

This means:

> Think about how the author made the story exciting. Why would you keep reading until the end of the story? Was there something exciting that you wanted to find out about? Give examples of the parts of the story that excited or interested you. Remember, if you can't think of anything that excites you about this particular passage, it's okay to pretend for the test!

Write, write, write, explain, explain, explain!

Name _____   **Evaluation: Narrative**

How did the author make you want to keep reading?

Vocabulary Box

how	
author	
make you want to keep reading	

Student-Friendly Translation

Explain how the author wrote the story to keep you reading. Tell how he or she wrote suspense, action, or surprise into the story.

This means:

Think about how the author made the story exciting. Why would you keep reading until the end of the story? Was there something exciting that you wanted to find out about? Give examples of the parts of the story that excited or interested you. Remember, if you can't think of anything that excites you about this particular passage, it's okay to pretend for the test!

Write, write, write, explain, explain, explain!

Name _____   **Evaluation: Narrative**

Tell how the author created the mood.

Vocabulary Box

tell how	tell more about, give examples of, describe, explain
author	the person who wrote the book
created	established, made
mood	atmosphere, vibe, general frame of mind, attitude

Student-Friendly Translation

> Explain what the author did to create the overall feeling of the passage. Give examples from the passage.

This means:

> Was the story bright and happy or dreary and depressing? What did the author do to make it that way? Did he or she have all the characters meet at a funeral of a friend of theirs or did the author set the story in a happier time? What did the characters say (dialogue)? What kinds of descriptions did the author include? These are all ways that the author made the mood or feeling of the passage. Be sure to include details from the passage to explain your ideas.

Write, write, write, explain, explain, explain!

Name _____   **Evaluation: Narrative**

Tell how the author created the mood.

Vocabulary Box

tell how	
author	
created	
mood	

Student-Friendly Translation

> Explain what the author did to create the overall feeling of the passage. Give examples from the passage.

This means:

> Was the story bright and happy or dreary and depressing? What did the author do to make it that way? Did he or she have all the characters meet at a funeral of a friend of theirs or did the author set the story in a happier time? What did the characters say (dialogue)? What kinds of descriptions did the author include? These are all ways that the author made the mood or feeling of the passage. Be sure to include details from the passage to explain your ideas.

Write, write, write, explain, explain, explain!

Name _____   **Evaluation: Narrative**

Why did the author write this piece?

Vocabulary Box

author	person who wrote the story or passage
piece	passage, story, selection

Student-Friendly Translation

Study the author's reasons for writing this book. (Making money is not the reason!) Why did he or she write this story instead of some other story?

This means:

Use examples from the passage to explain why this author wrote this book. Did he or she want to teach you something? Did he or she want to entertain you? If you have no idea, find examples in the book and make it up!

Write, write, write, explain, explain, explain!

Name _____   **Evaluation: Narrative**

Why did the author write this piece?

Vocabulary Box

author	
piece	

Student-Friendly Translation

Study the author's reasons for writing this book. (Making money is not the reason!) Why did he or she write this story instead of some other story?

This means:

Use examples from the passage to explain why this author wrote this book. Did he or she want to teach you something? Did he or she want to entertain you? If you have no idea, find examples in the book and make it up!

Write, write, write, explain, explain, explain!

Name _____   **Evaluation: Narrative**

If you were the main character, would you want the story to end the way it did?

Vocabulary Box

main character	most important person or animal
story	passage, selection

Student-Friendly Translation

Tell more about whether the main character would want the story finished in the way the author wrote it.

This means:

Describe and give examples of whether the main character in the story would like the ending the author wrote. Think about how the story ends. If you were the main character, would you want your story to end that way? Even if the story has a happy ending, do you think the character would like it? Think of other ways to end the story. Think about the character. Use examples from the story!

Write, write, write, explain, explain, explain!

Name _____   **Evaluation: Narrative**

If you were the main character, would you want the story to end the way it did?

Vocabulary Box

main character	
story	

Student-Friendly Translation

> Tell more about whether the main character would want the story finished in the way the author wrote it.

This means:

> Describe and give examples of whether the main character in the story would like the ending the author wrote. Think about how the story ends. If you were the main character, would you want your story to end that way? Even if the story has a happy ending, do you think the character would like it? Think of other ways to end the story. Think about the character. Use examples from the story!

Write, write, write, explain, explain, explain!

Name _____   **Evaluation: Narrative**

How did the author convey the feelings of the main character?

Vocabulary Box

how	explain, give examples, describe
author	the person who wrote the passage
convey	communicate, show, tell, describe, let you know
feelings of the main character	how the most important person or animal feels

Student-Friendly Translation

Explain how the author lets you know how the character feels.

This means:

Give examples from the story that show how the character feels. Does the author show the character punching something, which would make you know that the character is mad? Does the author have the character talk about his or her feelings to a friend or adult or does the author describe the character's face (for example: tears were streaming down Amber's face)? Does the author use descriptions, dialogue (characters talking), or action? Or does the author just write, Amber was really, really mad? Use details from the story to explain!

Write, write, write, explain, explain, explain!

Name _____   **Evaluation: Narrative**

How did the author convey the feelings of the main character?

Vocabulary Box

how	
author	
convey	
feelings of the main character	

Student-Friendly Translation

Explain how the author lets you know how the character feels.

This means:

Give examples from the story that show how the character feels. Does the author show the character punching something, which would make you know that the character is mad? Does the author have the character talk about his or her feelings to a friend or adult or does the author describe the character's face (for example: tears were streaming down Amber's face)? Does the author use descriptions, dialogue (characters talking), or action? Or does the author just write, Amber was really, really mad? Use details from the story to explain!

Write, write, write, explain, explain, explain!

Name _____   **Evaluation: Narrative**

How effective is the author in his or her word choice?

Vocabulary Box

effective	successful, useful, helpful, good
author	the person who wrote the book
word choice	vocabulary, using the right word for the meaning

Student-Friendly Translation

What do you think about the words the author used in this passage?

This means:

Did the author use the same words that you would use in this passage? Did he or she repeat the same words over and over? Was there a reason for the repetition or could the author have used other words? Were the words he or she used interesting? Give examples!

Write, write, write, explain, explain, explain!

Name _____   **Evaluation: Narrative**

How effective is the author in his or her word choice?

Vocabulary Box

effective	
author	
word choice	

Student-Friendly Translation

What do you think about the words the author used in this passage?

This means:

Did the author use the same words that you would use in this passage? Did he or she repeat the same words over and over? Was there a reason for the repetition or could the author have used other words? Were the words he or she used interesting? Give examples!

Write, write, write, explain, explain, explain!

Name _____ **Evaluation: Narrative**

How effective is the author in writing dialogue?

Vocabulary Box

effective	successful, useful, helpful
author	the person who wrote the book
dialogue	character's talk, conversation, speaking parts

Student-Friendly Translation

Check the success of the talking in the passage. What do you think about the speaking parts in the passage? Give examples from the passage to explain your ideas.

This means:

Locate the dialogue in the passage. It's surrounded by "quotation marks" and usually indented. Does it sound like real people talking? What could make it more real? Is it easy to understand what the characters are talking about? What could make it clearer? Explain what you think and use examples!

Write, write, write, explain, explain, explain!

Name _____   **Evaluation: Narrative**

How effective is the author in writing dialogue?

Vocabulary Box

effective	
author	
dialogue	

Student-Friendly Translation

> Check the success of the talking in the passage. What do you think about the speaking parts in the passage? Give examples from the passage to explain your ideas.

This means:

> Locate the dialogue in the passage. It's surrounded by "quotation marks" and usually indented. Does it sound like real people talking? What could make it more real? Is it easy to understand what the characters are talking about? What could make it clearer? Explain what you think and use examples!

Write, write, write, explain, explain, explain!

Name _____   **Evaluation: Narrative**

How effective is the author in describing the setting?

Vocabulary Box

effective	successful, useful, helpful
author	the person who wrote the book
setting	the place and time where the story happens

Student-Friendly Translation

> How well did the author do in describing the place and time where the story happens? Use examples from the passage to explain your ideas.

This means:

> Think about the place where the main part of the story happens: what is it like? Is the description clear? If you were the author, would you have described it differently? Explain what you think and use examples!

Write, write, write, explain, explain, explain!

Name _____   **Evaluation: Narrative**

How effective is the author in describing the setting?

Vocabulary Box

effective	
author	
setting	

Student-Friendly Translation

> How well did the author do in describing the place and time where the story happens? Use examples from the passage to explain your ideas.

This means:

> Think about the place where the main part of the story happens: what is it like? Is the description clear? If you were the author, would you have described it differently? Explain what you think and use examples!

Write, write, write, explain, explain, explain!

Name _____   **Evaluation: Narrative**

How effective is the author in characterization?

Vocabulary Box

effective	successful, useful, helpful
author	the person who wrote the book
characterization	character development, how characters are presented

Student-Friendly Translation

> How successful is the author in creating the characters? Use examples from the passage to explain your ideas.

This means:

> Think about the characters. How are they presented by the author? Are they introduced by what they say, what they think, or what they do? Or does the author/narrator tell you about the characters? If you were the author, would you have shown the characters differently? Explain what you think and use examples!

Write, write, write, explain, explain, explain!

Name _____   **Evaluation: Narrative**

How effective is the author in characterization?

Vocabulary Box

effective	
author	
characterization	

Student-Friendly Translation

> How successful is the author in creating the characters? Use examples from the passage to explain your ideas.

This means:

> Think about the characters. How are they presented by the author? Are they introduced by what they say, what they think, or what they do? Or does the author/narrator tell you about the characters? If you were the author, would you have shown the characters differently? Explain what you think and use examples!

Write, write, write, explain, explain, explain!

Name _____   **Evaluation: Narrative**

How effective is the author in creating the mood?

Vocabulary Box

effective	successful, useful, helpful
author	the person who wrote the book
mood	feeling, tone, atmosphere, frame of mind

Student-Friendly Translation

How successful is the author in describing the overall feeling of the passage? Use examples from the passage to explain your ideas.

This means:

Think about the mood of the story and characters: what is it like? Is it clearly described? If you were the author, would you have explained it differently? Explain what you think and use examples!

Write, write, write, explain, explain, explain!

Name _____   **Evaluation: Narrative**

How effective is the author in creating the mood?

Vocabulary Box

effective	
author	
mood	

Student-Friendly Translation

> How successful is the author in describing the overall feeling of the passage? Use examples from the passage to explain your ideas.

This means:

> Think about the mood of the story and characters: what is it like? Is it clearly described? If you were the author, would you have explained it differently? Explain what you think and use examples!

Write, write, write, explain, explain, explain!

Name _____   **Evaluation: Narrative**

How effective is the author in the use of text features?

Vocabulary Box

effective	successful, useful, helpful
author	the person who wrote the book
use of text features	use of pictures, drawings, photographs, illustrations

Student-Friendly Translation

How successful is the author in using pictures and drawings in the passage? Use examples from the passage to explain your ideas.

This means:

Think about the pictures. How are they presented? Would you have used different pictures or scenes if you were making the book? Are there pictures of the exciting parts? Explain what you think and use examples!

Write, write, write, explain, explain, explain!

Name _____   **Evaluation: Narrative**

How effective is the author in the use of text features?

Vocabulary Box

effective	
author	
use of text features	

Student-Friendly Translation

> How successful is the author in using pictures and drawings in the passage? Use examples from the passage to explain your ideas.

This means:

> Think about the pictures. How are they presented? Would you have used different pictures or scenes if you were making the book? Are there pictures of the exciting parts? Explain what you think and use examples!

Write, write, write, explain, explain, explain!

Name _____   **Evaluation: Narrative**

Did the sequence of events make sense?

Vocabulary Box

sequence	order, cycle, progression, chain
events	things that happened in the story

Student-Friendly Translation

What did you think about the way the story or piece was put together? Did it seem organized? Use examples from the passage to explain your ideas.

This means:

How was the story or passage organized? Were there flashbacks or flash-forwards? Did the story begin at an exciting part and then explain how it all started? Did the organization make sense? Explain what you think and use examples!

Write, write, write, explain, explain, explain!

Name _____   **Evaluation: Narrative**

Did the sequence of events make sense?

Vocabulary Box

sequence	
events	

Student-Friendly Translation

> What did you think about the way the story or piece was put together? Did it seem organized? Use examples from the passage to explain your ideas.

This means:

> How was the story or passage organized? Were there flashbacks or flash-forwards? Did the story begin at an exciting part and then explain how it all started? Did the organization make sense? Explain what you think and use examples!

Write, write, write, explain, explain, explain!

Name _____   **Evaluation: Narrative**

How does the author's choice of setting impact the characters?

Vocabulary Box

how does	give examples of, state an opinion about
setting	place where and time when the story happens
impact	influence, affect, make a difference
characters	main people or animals in the story

Student-Friendly Translation

> Give examples of how the time and place of the story make a difference in the people or animals in the story. Give examples from the story!

This means:

> Could these characters be the same in a different place or time? How important is the setting to the story and the character development? Don't forget to give examples from the passage to support your opinion!

Write, write, write, explain, explain, explain!

Name _____   **Evaluation: Narrative**

How does the author's choice of setting impact the characters?

Vocabulary Box

how does	
setting	
impact	
characters	

Student-Friendly Translation

> Give examples of how the time and place of the story make a difference in the people or animals in the story. Give examples from the story!

This means:

> Could these characters be the same in a different place or time? How important is the setting to the story and the character development? Don't forget to give examples from the passage to support your opinion!

Write, write, write, explain, explain, explain!

Name _____   **Evaluation: Narrative**

Is the setting realistic or fantastic?

Vocabulary Box

setting	place where the story happens
realistic	like real life, it could happen
fantastic	from fantasy, things that could not really happen in life

Student-Friendly Translation

Tell whether you think the place in the story could really be a place in life. Give examples from the story!

This means:

Does the setting seem like a real place? Is there something in the setting that could not happen in real life? It's okay to say that the setting is realistic, but don't forget to give examples from the passage to support your opinion!

Write, write, write, explain, explain, explain!

Name _____   **Evaluation: Narrative**

Is the setting realistic or fantastic?

Vocabulary Box

setting	
realistic	
fantastic	

Student-Friendly Translation

> Tell whether you think the place in the story could really be a place in life. Give examples from the story!

This means:

> Does the setting seem like a real place? Is there something in the setting that could not happen in real life? It's okay to say that the setting is realistic, but don't forget to give examples from the passage to support your opinion!

Write, write, write, explain, explain, explain!

Name _____   **Evaluation: Narrative**

How does the author show that the story is fantasy?

Vocabulary Box

author	the person who wrote the story
fantasy	the type of story in which things happen that can't happen in real life on Earth; usually involves magic

Student-Friendly Translation

> How does the person who wrote the story show that the story can't happen in real life on Earth?

This means:

> There are many genres in fiction. Science fiction and fantasy are similar because they include setting, actions, plot, or characters that couldn't be found in realistic fiction. Science fiction uses story elements associated with science and the future. Fantasy uses story elements involving magic and other mythic phenomena. What story elements (characters, setting, or actions) in this story involve magic or other fantastic things? Be sure to include details from the story.

Write, write, write, explain, explain, explain!

Name _____   **Evaluation: Narrative**

How does the author show that the story is fantasy?

Vocabulary Box

author	
fantasy	

Student-Friendly Translation

> How does the person who wrote the story show that the story can't happen in real life on Earth?

This means:

> There are many genres in fiction. Science fiction and fantasy are similar because they include setting, actions, plot, or characters that couldn't be found in realistic fiction. Science fiction uses story elements associated with science and the future. Fantasy uses story elements involving magic and other mythic phenomena. What story elements (characters, setting, or actions) in this story involve magic or other fantastic things? Be sure to include details from the story.

Write, write, write, explain, explain, explain!

Name _____   **Evaluation: Narrative**

Are the characters realistic?

Vocabulary Box

characters	people or animals in the story
realistic	real, lifelike, true, accurate

Student-Friendly Translation

Are the people or animals in the story lifelike?

This means:

Do the people or animals in the story do things that people or animals do in real life? If the people fly or if the animals talk, you know for sure that they are not realistic, but you can also judge the characters on another level. Do they say and do things that you think they would do? For instance, if the policeman character in a book is more like a friend in what he does or says, you could say that the character isn't realistic, because policemen need to be professional and more authoritative than a friend. Be sure to include details from the passage to show why you think the characters in the story are realistic or not.

Write, write, write, explain, explain, explain!

Name _____   **Evaluation: Narrative**

Are the characters realistic?

Vocabulary Box

characters	
realistic	

Student-Friendly Translation

Are the people or animals in the story lifelike?

This means:

Do the people or animals in the story do things that people or animals do in real life? If the people fly or if the animals talk, you know for sure that they are not realistic, but you can also judge the characters on another level. Do they say and do things that you think they would do? For instance, if the policeman character in a book is more like a friend in what he does or says, you could say that the character isn't realistic, because policemen need to be professional and more authoritative than a friend. Be sure to include details from the passage to show why you think the characters in the story are realistic or not.

Write, write, write, explain, explain, explain!

Name _____   **Evaluation: Narrative**

How did the author make the story seem like it could happen?

Vocabulary Box

author	person who wrote the passage
story	passage, selection, piece
seem like it could happen	realistic, accurate, lifelike

Student-Friendly Translation

How did the person who wrote the passage make it lifelike?

This means:

What did the person who wrote the passage do to make the passage realistic? The author creates the whole story, so you could talk about how realistic the characters are. Do they really seem like real people to you? Is it what they say or do? You could also discuss how realistic the setting is. Does it seem like a real place to you? How does the author describe it? You could also talk about how the plot, problem, and solution seem like things that could really happen. The most important thing is to clearly answer the question and to give examples from the story to support your answer.

Write, write, write, explain, explain, explain!

Name _____   **Evaluation: Narrative**

How did the author make the story seem like it could happen?

Vocabulary Box

author	
story	
seem like it could happen	

Student-Friendly Translation

How did the person who wrote the passage make it lifelike?

This means:

What did the person who wrote the passage do to make the passage realistic? The author creates the whole story, so you could talk about how realistic the characters are. Do they really seem like real people to you? Is it what they say or do? You could also discuss how realistic the setting is. Does it seem like a real place to you? How does the author describe it? You could also talk about how the plot, problem, and solution seem like things that could really happen. The most important thing is to clearly answer the question and to give examples from the story to support your answer.

Write, write, write, explain, explain, explain!

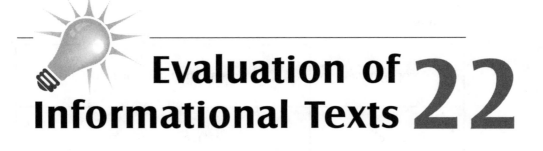

Evaluation of Informational Texts 22

Name _____   **Evaluation: Informational**

Find propaganda in this article.

Vocabulary Box

propaganda	misinformation, half-truths
article	passage, text, selection

Student-Friendly Translation

Find information in the text that isn't completely true, but is written by people for a purpose.

This means:

Propaganda sounds true because it is said with such power. What information in this passage doesn't sound quite right to you? Why? Give details from the piece to explain your point.

Write, write, write, explain, explain, explain!

Name _____　　　**Evaluation: Informational**

Find propaganda in this article.

Vocabulary Box

propaganda	
article	

Student-Friendly Translation

> Find information in the text that isn't completely true, but is written by people for a purpose.

This means:

> Propaganda sounds true because it is said with such power. What information in this passage doesn't sound quite right to you? Why? Give details from the piece to explain your point.

Write, write, write, explain, explain, explain!

Name _____   **Evaluation: Informational**

Point out the author's bias in this article.

Vocabulary Box

point out	find, show, give examples of
author's bias	hidden feelings of the author, the writer's prejudice
article	passage, piece of writing

Student-Friendly Translation

Give examples of the writer's personal hidden feelings in this passage.

This means:

Try to read "between the lines" to figure out how the author really feels about this subject. Everyone has feelings about subjects they write about that they may try to hide. A student writing an essay about the benefits of homework may mention details about the benefits of short homework assignments. That student has hidden feelings about the subject. Those hidden feelings are called a bias. Find information about the author to help discover his or her possible bias.

Write, write, write, explain, explain, explain!

Name _____   **Evaluation: Informational**

Point out the author's bias in this article.

Vocabulary Box

point out	
author's bias	
article	

Student-Friendly Translation

Give examples of the writer's personal hidden feelings in this passage.

This means:

Try to read "between the lines" to figure out how the author really feels about this subject. Everyone has feelings about subjects they write about that they may try to hide. A student writing an essay about the benefits of homework may mention details about the benefits of short homework assignments. That student has hidden feelings about the subject. Those hidden feelings are called a bias. Find information about the author to help discover his or her possible bias.

Write, write, write, explain, explain, explain!

Name _____   **Evaluation: Informational**

Evaluate the clarity of the text.

Vocabulary Box

evaluate	determine, choose, make a decision about
clarity	how clearly, how well, how understandably
text	passage, facts, data

Student-Friendly Translation

> Make a decision about how well the facts in the passage were introduced. Think about the clearness of the writing. Give examples from the passage!

This means:

> What facts and information is the author trying to tell you? Did he or she do a good job of it? How could the author have done it more clearly? It's okay to say that the author did a good job, but you must include examples from the passage.

Write, write, write, explain, explain, explain!

Name _____   **Evaluation: Informational**

Evaluate the clarity of the text.

Vocabulary Box

evaluate	
clarity	
text	

Student-Friendly Translation

Make a decision about how well the facts in the passage were introduced. Think about the clearness of the writing. Give examples from the passage!

This means:

What facts and information is the author trying to tell you? Did he or she do a good job of it? How could the author have done it more clearly? It's okay to say that the author did a good job, but you must include examples from the passage.

Write, write, write, explain, explain, explain!

Name _____   **Evaluation: Informational**

Evaluate the usefulness of this piece for learning about the topic.

Vocabulary Box

evaluate	make a decision about, appraise, give details
usefulness	the value, helpfulness
this piece	this passage or book
learning	finding out
the topic	the subject, the main idea of the passage

Student-Friendly Translation

Tell more about how helpful this passage is for finding out about the subject of the passage. Give examples!

This means:

What was the passage or book mainly about? Did you learn new things? How helpful would this book be for someone who was doing research on the subject? It's okay to say that the author did a good job, but you must include examples from the passage.

Write, write, write, explain, explain, explain!

Name _____   **Evaluation: Informational**

Evaluate the usefulness of this piece for learning about the topic.

Vocabulary Box

evaluate	
usefulness	
this piece	
learning	
the topic	

Student-Friendly Translation

Tell more about how helpful this passage is for finding out about the subject of the passage. Give examples!

This means:

What was the passage or book mainly about? Did you learn new things? How helpful would this book be for someone who was doing research on the subject? It's okay to say that the author did a good job, but you must include examples from the passage.

Write, write, write, explain, explain, explain!

Name _____   **Evaluation: Informational**

What text features does the author use to make the passage easier to read?

Vocabulary Box

describe	tell about, give examples, explain
text	article, piece of writing
features	title, subtitles, pictures, drawings, maps, charts, anything besides plain writing
author	the person who wrote the article

Student-Friendly Translation

> Tell about the title, subtitles, pictures, charts, or other things besides the regular sentences that the writer used to make the article easier to read.

This means:

> Notice everything on the page in addition to the words. Are there pictures, drawings, graphs, charts, or maps? Does the article have a title? Are there subtitles to draw your attention to special parts? Notice how those features help you understand the article better. Explain using details from the passage.

Write, write, write, explain, explain, explain!

Name _____   **Evaluation: Informational**

What text features does the author use to make the passage easier to read?

Vocabulary Box

describe	
text	
features	
author	

Student-Friendly Translation

Tell about the title, subtitles, pictures, charts, or other things besides the regular sentences that the writer used to make the article easier to read.

This means:

Notice everything on the page in addition to the words. Are there pictures, drawings, graphs, charts, or maps? Does the article have a title? Are there subtitles to draw your attention to special parts? Notice how those features help you understand the article better. Explain using details from the passage.

Write, write, write, explain, explain, explain!

Name _____   **Evaluation: Informational**

How accurate is the information in this article?

Vocabulary Box

accurate	true, correct, right
information	what you read
article	passage, selection

Student-Friendly Translation

> Tell whether you think the article is correct and give examples that show why or why not.

This means:

> Think about anything you know about the subject. Does the information in this article make sense, based on what you know? What if you don't know anything about the subject of this passage? It is okay to make up a reasonable story.

Write, write, write, explain, explain, explain!

Name _____   **Evaluation: Informational**

How accurate is the information in this article?

Vocabulary Box

accurate	
information	
article	

Student-Friendly Translation

Tell whether you think the article is correct and give examples that show why or why not.

This means:

Think about anything you know about the subject. Does the information in this article make sense, based on what you know? What if you don't know anything about the subject of this passage? It is okay to make up a reasonable story.

Write, write, write, explain, explain, explain!

Name _____   **Evaluation: Informational**

How do you know the author is qualified to write this article?

Vocabulary Box

author	the person who wrote this article
qualified	knows enough to explain the topic, has experience or training in the subject
article	piece, passage, reading

Student-Friendly Translation

> How do you know that the person who wrote this passage knows enough to write it? Give examples from the article to make it clear.

This means:

> If you were going to write this article, what would you have to know? What are some specific things the author had to know to write this article? How do you think he or she learned them? Remember to give details from the article that show that the author is qualified to write it.

Write, write, write, explain, explain, explain!

Name _____   **Evaluation: Informational**

How do you know the author is qualified to write this article?

Vocabulary Box

author	
qualified	
article	

Student-Friendly Translation

> How do you know that the person who wrote this passage knows
> enough to write it? Give examples from the article to make it clear.

This means:

> If you were going to write this article, what would you have to know?
> What are some specific things the author had to know to write this
> article? How do you think he or she learned them? Remember to give
> details from the article that show that the author is qualified to write it.

Write, write, write, explain, explain, explain!

Name _____   **Evaluation: Informational**

Why do you think the author wrote this article?

Vocabulary Box

why	point out, show, find
do you think	give your own opinion
author	person who wrote the passage

Student-Friendly Translation

Point out the person who wrote the passage's reason for writing it.

This means:

Think about the passage. Why did the author write it? Did he or she want to teach people about something or entertain them? Think about why someone would write this. "To make money or be famous" are not good answers. This author could have written many other things but chose to write this; why? Be sure to include lots of details from the passage.

Write, write, write, explain, explain, explain!

Name _____   **Evaluation: Informational**

Why do you think the author wrote this article?

Vocabulary Box

why	
do you think	
author	

Student-Friendly Translation

Point out the person who wrote the passage's reason for writing it.

This means:

Think about the passage. Why did the author write it? Did he or she want to teach people about something or entertain them? Think about why someone would write this. "To make money or be famous" are not good answers. This author could have written many other things but chose to write this; why? Be sure to include lots of details from the passage.

Write, write, write, explain, explain, explain!

Name _____ **Evaluation: Informational**

Tell how someone would use this information.

Vocabulary Box

tell how	point out, give details about, identify
use	apply, bring into play, make use of
information	facts, details

Student-Friendly Translation

Tell who would apply these facts and what that person would do with them.

This means:

Think about who would need this information. What kind of person would need to know this? Think of jobs people do where they might need to know these things. Use details from the story to connect the people and the information. Explain what those people could do with this information.

Write, write, write, explain, explain, explain!

Name _____   **Evaluation: Informational**

Tell how someone would use this information.

Vocabulary Box

tell how	
use	
information	

Student-Friendly Translation

Tell who would apply these facts and what that person would do with them.

This means:

Think about who would need this information. What kind of person would need to know this? Think of jobs people do where they might need to know these things. Use details from the story to connect the people and the information. Explain what those people could do with this information.

Write, write, write, explain, explain, explain!

Name _____   **Evaluation: Informational**

What part shows the author's point of view?

Vocabulary Box

part	facts, details, information
shows	communicates, expresses, gives
author's	the person who wrote the passage
point of view	way of looking at things, opinions, ideas

Student-Friendly Translation

> What information shows the opinion of the person who wrote this passage?

This means:

> Think about what the person who wrote this passage might think about the subject. Sometimes this is very clear because the author is trying to convince you about something. Sometimes it isn't clear, but the author chose to write about this subject for a reason. People write about things they feel strongly about, either because they like those things or because they don't. Does the author talk about the people in this piece as if the author admires them? Find clues to the author's way of looking at things, state your opinion clearly in your thesis statement, and give details to support your ideas.

Write, write, write, explain, explain, explain!

Name _____   **Evaluation: Informational**

What part shows the author's point of view?

Vocabulary Box

part	
shows	
author's	
point of view	

Student-Friendly Translation

What information shows the opinion of the person who wrote this passage?

This means:

Think about what the person who wrote this passage might think about the subject. Sometimes this is very clear because the author is trying to convince you about something. Sometimes it isn't clear, but the author chose to write about this subject for a reason. People write about things they feel strongly about, either because they like those things or because they don't. Does the author talk about the people in this piece as if the author admires them? Find clues to the author's way of looking at things, state your opinion clearly in your thesis statement, and give details to support your ideas.

Write, write, write, explain, explain, explain!

Name _____   **Evaluation: Informational**

After reading two passages on the same topic, choose which one presents the information more clearly.

Vocabulary Box

two passages	two articles, texts, or selections
same topic	same subject, about the same thing
choose which	decide, evaluate, pick one
presents	gives, shows, explains
information	facts, details
more clearly	with the best clarity, in the best way, simplest to understand

Student-Friendly Translation

Looking at two articles about the same subject, choose one that explains the facts so they are easy and clear to understand.

This means:

Which piece makes the most sense to you? Which is the easiest to understand? Are there any parts that are unclear or confusing? Point out the parts that are easy to understand and those that are confusing. Be sure to take a clear stance and choose the one that is clear. Tell why one is clear and the other is unclear. Give examples!

Write, write, write, explain, explain, explain!

Name _____   **Evaluation: Informational**

After reading two passages on the same topic, choose which one presents the information more clearly.

Vocabulary Box

two passages	
same topic	
choose which	
presents	
information	
more clearly	

Student-Friendly Translation

Looking at two articles about the same subject, choose one that explains the facts so they are easy and clear to understand.

This means:

Which piece makes the most sense to you? Which is the easiest to understand? Are there any parts that are unclear or confusing? Point out the parts that are easy to understand and those that are confusing. Be sure to take a clear stance and choose the one that is clear. Tell why one is clear and the other is unclear. Give examples!

Write, write, write, explain, explain, explain!

Evaluation of Functional Texts 23

Name _____   **Evaluation: Functional**

How important are the graphics to your understanding of the whole passage?

Vocabulary Box

graphics	pictures, charts, drawings, any text features other than plain words
understanding of the whole passage	being able to follow the directions, do the assigned activity

Student-Friendly Translation

How do the pictures, charts, or drawings help you (the reader) do the activity described in the directions?

This means:

How do the pictures of the job help you understand the job? Imagine what pictures, charts, or drawings you would include if you were writing this piece. How can pictures help the reader understand? Be sure to give details from the passage to explain your ideas.

Write, write, write, explain, explain, explain!

Name _____   **Evaluation: Functional**

How important are the graphics to your understanding of the whole passage?

Vocabulary Box

graphics	
understanding of the whole passage	

Student-Friendly Translation

> How do the pictures, charts, or drawings help you (the reader) do the activity described in the directions?

This means:

> How do the pictures of the job help you understand the job? Imagine what pictures, charts, or drawings you would include if you were writing this piece. How can pictures help the reader understand? Be sure to give details from the passage to explain your ideas.

Write, write, write, explain, explain, explain!

Name _____   **Evaluation: Functional**

Do you have to do the steps in order?

Vocabulary Box

steps	procedures, actions, list items
order	the way the actions are listed here

Student-Friendly Translation

Does it make a difference if you do the actions out of order? Why or why not?

This means:

Think what would happen if you did the middle step first or last. Would it change the end result? Most things have to be done in a certain order, but not all things. Is this something that has an order, or not? Be sure to include details about why it is or why it is not.

Write, write, write, explain, explain, explain!

Name _____   **Evaluation: Functional**

Do you have to do the steps in order?

Vocabulary Box

steps	
order	

Student-Friendly Translation

> Does it make a difference if you do the actions out of order? Why or why not?

This means:

> Think what would happen if you did the middle step first or last. Would it change the end result? Most things have to be done in a certain order, but not all things. Is this something that has an order, or not? Be sure to include details about why it is or why it is not.

Write, write, write, explain, explain, explain!

Name _____   **Evaluation: Functional**

How could the author make the information easier to understand?

Vocabulary Box

author	person who wrote the passage
information	details
easier	better, simpler

Student-Friendly Translation

Point out things that are confusing about the information. Use details from the passage to explain.

This means:

Even if you totally understand the information, find some parts that could be confusing to another reader. Point out these parts and tell what is confusing and how it could be clearer. Give details to make your points clear.

Write, write, write, explain, explain, explain!

Name _____   **Evaluation: Functional**

How could the author make the information easier to understand?

Vocabulary Box

author	
information	
easier	

Student-Friendly Translation

Point out things that are confusing about the information. Use details from the passage to explain.

This means:

Even if you totally understand the information, find some parts that could be confusing to another reader. Point out these parts and tell what is confusing and how it could be clearer. Give details to make your points clear.

Write, write, write, explain, explain, explain!

Name _____   **Evaluation: Functional**

What recommendations would you make to the author to improve the directions?

Vocabulary Box

recommendations	suggestions, advice
author	writer
improve	change to make better
directions	instructions, steps

Student-Friendly Translation

What suggestions would you give the writer to make the instructions better?

This means:

Think about what could be changed in the directions. What could you change about the instructions? Are they clear? Are they easy enough to understand? Think about the job the directions are explaining. Can you figure out how to do it? What would help? Be sure to include details from the directions as you are giving your advice.

Write, write, write, explain, explain, explain!

Name _____   **Evaluation: Functional**

What recommendations would you make to the author to improve the directions?

Vocabulary Box

recommendations	
author	
improve	
directions	

Student-Friendly Translation

> What suggestions would you give the writer to make the instructions better?

This means:

> Think about what could be changed in the directions. What could you change about the instructions? Are they clear? Are they easy enough to understand? Think about the job the directions are explaining. Can you figure out how to do it? What would help? Be sure to include details from the directions as you are giving your advice.

Write, write, write, explain, explain, explain!

Name _____   **Evaluation: Functional**

How useful is this passage?

Vocabulary Box

useful	worthwhile, helpful, effective
passage	piece, article, selection

Student-Friendly Translation

How helpful is this selection?

This means:

Is this passage helpful or useful to you or another reader? Explain your opinion using details from the passage to support your ideas. Pretend you asked someone to write this for you. Did he or she do a good job of making it useful for you? Be sure to include details from the passage.

Write, write, write, explain, explain, explain!

Name _____   **Evaluation: Functional**

How useful is this passage?

Vocabulary Box

useful	
passage	

Student-Friendly Translation

How helpful is this selection?

This means:

Is this passage helpful or useful to you or another reader? Explain your opinion using details from the passage to support your ideas. Pretend you asked someone to write this for you. Did he or she do a good job of making it useful for you? Be sure to include details from the passage.

Write, write, write, explain, explain, explain!

Name _____   **Evaluation: Functional**

Identify points of confusion in the instructions.

Vocabulary Box

identify	point out, give details about
points of confusion	things that are confusing
instructions	directions, information

Student-Friendly Translation

> Point out things that are confusing about the facts and details. Use details from the passage to explain.

This means:

> Even if you totally understand the facts, find some parts that could be confusing to another reader. Point out these parts and tell what is confusing and how it could be clearer. Give details to make your points clear.

Write, write, write, explain, explain, explain!

Name _____   **Evaluation: Functional**

Identify points of confusion in the instructions.

Vocabulary Box

identify	
points of confusion	
instructions	

Student-Friendly Translation

Point out things that are confusing about the facts and details. Use details from the passage to explain.

This means:

Even if you totally understand the facts, find some parts that could be confusing to another reader. Point out these parts and tell what is confusing and how it could be clearer. Give details to make your points clear.

Write, write, write, explain, explain, explain!

Resources

Picture Books

Aardema, V. (1975). Why mosquitoes buzz in people's ears. New York: Dial Press.

Baylor, B. (1987). *The desert is theirs*. New York: Aladdin.

Berenstain, S., & Berenstain, J. (1984). *The Berenstain bears and too much TV*. New York: Random House.

Berenstain, S., & Berenstain, J. (1987). *The Berenstain bears and the trouble with friends*. New York: Random House.

Brown, M. (1996a). *Arthur and the true Francine*. Boston: Little, Brown.

Brown, M. (1996b). *Arthur writes a story*. Boston: Little, Brown.

Bunting, E. (1990). *The wall*. New York: Clarion Books.

Bunting, E. (1999). *Smoky night*. New York: Voyager Books.

Chandra, D., & Comora, M. (2003). *George Washington's teeth*. New York: Farrar, Straus, & Giroux.

Charles, V. (1992). *The crane girl*. Toronto: Oxford University Press.

Child, L. (2003). *I will never not ever eat a tomato*. Cambridge, MA: Candlewick Press.

Creech, S. (2001). *A fine, fine school*. New York: Joanna Cotler Books.

Finley, W. (2003). The water-horse of Barra. *Junior Great Books Series 4, First Semester*. Chicago: Great Books Foundation.

Harris, R. (1999). *Owlbert*. New York: Houghton Mifflin.

Hoffman, M. (1991). *Amazing Grace*. New York: Dial.

Johnson, D.B. (2000). *Henry hikes to Fitchberg*. Boston: Houghton Mifflin.

Keller, J. (1989). *Tom Edison's bright ideas*. Milwaukee, WI: Raintree Publishers.

Lang, G. (2001). *Looking out for Sarah*. Watertown, MA: Talewinds.

LeBox, A. (2000). *Wild bog tea*. Toronto, Canada: Groundwood Books.

Leedy, L. (1992). *Blast off to Earth! A look at geography*. New York: Holiday House.

Lewin, T. (2001). *Red legs*. New York: HarperCollins.

Marshall, J. (1977). *Miss Nelson is missing*. Boston: Houghton Mifflin.

Muth, J. (2003). *Stone soup*. New York: Scholastic Press.

Muth, J. (2005). *Zen shorts*. New York: Scholastic Press.

Myers, T. (2003). *Tanuki's gift*. New York: Marshall Cavendish.

Nolen, J. (1998). *Raising dragons.* San Diego, CA: Silver Whistle.

O'Neill, A. (2002). *The recess queen.* New York: Scholastic Press.

Rathman, P. (1995). *Officer Buckle and Gloria.* New York: Putnam.

Ringgold, F. (1991). *Tar beach.* New York: Crown.

Rylant, C. (1982). *When I was young in the mountains.* New York: Dutton.

Rylant, C. (1985). *Relatives came.* New York: Bradbury Press.

Rylant, C. (1995). *Dog heaven.* New York: Blue Sky Press.

Rylant, C. (2001). *The great Gracie chase.* New York: Blue Sky Press.

Say, A. (1993). *Grandfather's journey.* Boston: Houghton Mifflin.

Steig, W. (1969). *Sylvester and the magic pebble.* New York: Windmill Books.

Van Allsburg, C. (1985). *Polar express.* New York: Houghton Mifflin.

Viorst, J. (1989). *Alexander and the terrible, horrible, no good, very bad day.* New York: Simon and Schuster.

Wegler, M. (1999). *Rabbits.* New York: Barron's Educational Series.

Chapter Books

Christopher, M. (1970). *Johnny long legs.* Boston: Little, Brown.

Cleary, B. (1990). *The mouse and the motorcycle.* New York: Avon Books.

Creech, S. (1997). *Chasing Redbird.* New York: HarperCollins.

Dahl, R. (1972). *Charlie and the great glass elevator.* New York: Knopf.

Gardiner, J. (1980). *Stone fox.* New York: Harper & Row.

George, J. C. (1990). *On the far side of the mountain.* New York: Puffin Books.

Jordan, S. (2000). *Secret sacrament.* New York: HarperCollins.

Orwell, G. (1996). *Animal farm.* New York: Signet Books.

Paterson, K. (1978). *The great Gilly Hopkins.* New York: Crowell.

Paulsen, G. (1991). *The river.* New York: Delacorte Press.

Paulsen, G. (1993). *Night John.* New York: Delacorte Press.

Richards, P. (2004, January). Persistence. *Highlights for Children.* Honesdale, PA: Highlights for Children.

Rowling, J. K. (1999). *Harry Potter and the chamber of secrets.* New York: Arthur A. Levine Books.

Sachar, L. (1998). *Holes.* New York: Farrar, Straus, & Giroux.

Strasser, T. (2003). *Thief of dreams.* New York: G. P. Putnam's Sons.

Thomas, S. (1995). *Full house: Stephanie.* New York: Pocket Books.

Trueman, T. (2004). *Cruise control.* New York: HarperTempest.

Walsh, J. (1961). *The first book of physical fitness.* New York: Franklin Watts.

White, E. B. (1952). *Charlotte's web.* New York: Harper.

Professional References

Au, K., Carroll, J., & Scheu, J. (2001). *Balanced literacy instruction: A teacher's resource book.* Norwood, MA: Christopher-Gordon.

Bizar, M., & Daniels, H. (1998). *Methods that matter: Six structures for best practice classrooms.* Portland, ME: Stenhouse.

Cameron, C., Davies, A., & Gregory, K. (2000). *Self-assessment and goal-setting*. Courtenay, Canada: Connections.

Fletcher, R., & Portalupi, J. (1998). *Craft lessons: Teaching writing K–8*. Portland, ME: Stenhouse.

Rief, L. (1992). *Seeking diversity*. Portsmouth, NH: Heinemann.

Routman, R. (2003). *Reading essentials: The specifics you need to teach reading well*. Portsmouth, NH: Heinemann.

Spandel, V. (2001). *Books, lessons, ideas for teaching the six traits*. Wilmington, MA: Write Traits, Great Source Education Group.

Spandel, V. (2005). *Creating writers through 6-trait writing assessment and instruction* (4th ed.). Boston: Pearson Education.

Index

Fabulous Paper Gliders

Norman Schmidt

SCHOLASTIC INC.

New York Toronto London Auckland Sydney

Design: Norman Schmidt
Photography: Jerry Grajewski, Custom Images

ISBN 0-590-65392-X

12 11 10 9 8 7 6 5 4 3 2 1   9/9 0 1 2 3 4/0

Printed in the U.S.A.   14

First Scholastic printing, February 1999

Contents

Below: A typical scene at a gliderport. Shown on the flightline are various types of gliders preparing for launch.

Inset: Gliders are not large, most are single seat aircraft having a slender and streamlined profile. Shown is the author with his Schweizer SGS 1-26B

MANY people are familiar with the story of general aviation, beginning with the historic flight of the Wright brothers in 1903. Motorless flight, however, is less well known, in spite of the fact that motorless planes played a central role in the advent of aviation.

Motorless planes can perform two related kinds of flight — gliding and soaring. If you have ever tossed a paper plane into the air and watched it descend you observed gliding flight. In gliding flight a plane descends gradually forward and downward because the force of gravity pulls it earthward while at the same time the wings generate a lifting force to counteract the gravitational pull to buoy up the weight of the craft.

Soaring occurs when a plane in gliding flight encounters air currents that are rising faster than the glider is descending. These sources of lift (air currents) happen at various locations under certain meteorological conditions. Motorless planes or gliders that are specifically designed to soar are called sailplanes. They are to powered airplanes what sailboats are to motorboats.

As long ago as 1799, Sir George Cayley, an English inventor, was experimenting with small kite-like model airplanes made of paper and wood. Later he developed them into large planes that were capable of carrying a human being. Paper planes have continued to be popular ever since and have developed in their own right, increasing in efficiency and maximizing the aerodynamics of small sizes, light weight,

and low speed. An example of such a paper glider is the first model in this book, called The Paperwing. **(Paper glider 1, p 10.)**

Full-sized gliders have also evolved from primitive machines in Cayley's day, to sophisticated ones today. There are now scores of different types, classified according to performance level. One class is the Standard Class, of which the Libelle 201 is a good example. This sailplane has been built in greater numbers than any other in that class. **(Paper glider 2, p 14.)**

Gliders are truly fabulous flyers that have chalked up impressive flight records: namely more than 24 hours in the air at one time, over 1000 miles (1600 km) traveled in a single flight, and altitude gains of over 45,000 feet (13,500 m). If you don't have your own full-sized glider you can build a small-scale paper one and perhaps set some records with it. These tiny paper replicas can glide and soar, sometimes remaining airborne for a minute or more, sometimes catching an up-draft and soaring out of sight never to be seen again.

The paper gliders in this book trace the story of motorless flight as the glider developed in design and efficiency. They are modeled on gliders that have a distinctive place in motorless flight history. The planes are made from ordinary index card stock. All can be constructed by anyone having basic craft skills, allowing young and old to experience the thrill of flight firsthand.

NOTE: The proportions of the gliders and sailplanes represented in this book have been slightly altered in the paper models to suit the paper medium, and they are not in scale to each other.

General assembly instructions for the planes in this book

If you have not cut paper with a craft knife, begin by making some practice cuts. In pencil draw some squares, triangles, and circles of various sizes on index card stock and cut them out. For straight cuts use a steel edged ruler to guide the knife; make freehand cuts for curved lines. Always cut by drawing the knife towards you and away from the hand used to hold the paper. Continue until you are comfortable with the tools.

Use a sharp craft knife (an X-acto knife with a #11 blade) on a suitable cutting surface (an Olfa cutting mat). Practice cutting precisely on the line. Always keep the blade sharp.

The paper gliders in this book are constructed with three main parts made up of smaller cut out pieces built up in layers: (1) fuselage with vertical stabilizer, (2) wings, and (3) horizontal stabilizer.

Nothing is cut out of the book. Instead, make a photocopy of each of the pages containing glider parts. Then, on each photocopy, cut out the center portion (the parts layout). This makes it fit index card stock. Finally tack-glue this portion to card stock and use it as a cutting guide.

Index card tends to curl in one direction. Tack glue the cutting guide to the *convex* side of the card.

Cut through both the tacked on guide paper and the card stock underneath. Remove the part and discard the guide paper. This leaves a clean unmarked glider part, ready for assembly.

For all the cut out pieces, the side that faces up for cutting will be outward or upward facing on the finished glider. This is important for aerodynamic and aesthetic reasons because of the burr on the edges due to cutting.

For assembly, follow the detailed instructions given for each glider type. *Align parts carefully* . Take care to position the bent over parts accurately because they are the fastening tabs for wings and horizontal stabilizer.

GLUING

Stick glue (e.g. Uhu Color Stic), white craft glue, or wood-type model airplane glue can be used. However, it is easier to manage the drying time and reduce warpage with stick glue.

When building up the main parts in layers, apply glue to the entire *smaller* surface to be fastened to a larger one. Press parts firmly together. Continue until the entire main part is done.

Lay the assembled fuselage flat between clean sheets of paper underneath a weight (some heavy books) until the glue is sufficiently set. This will take between 30 and 45 minutes for stick glue, and several hours for white glue.

Discarded remains after the parts have been cut out.

The dihedral angle (upward slanting) of the wings must be adjusted while the parts are being assembled (before the glue is set). Use the angle guide given with each model. If stick glue is used, simply stand the wings on the leading edge (front edge) until the glue has set. If white glue (or model glue) is used, drying the wings is complicated. Some means must be devised to keep each wing from warping while maintaining the dihedral angle.

ADDING DETAILS

Make the cockpit canopy gray using a felt marker or soft pencil. Make wheels and skids black on gliders that have them. Add other details such as outlines for control surfaces with a soft pencil.

Full-scale gliders are predominantly white because many are of composite construction. Such gliders are heat sensitive, losing structural strength as they become heated.

White reflects the rays of the sun and the gliders remain cool. Gliders made of other materials are also often white to keep them cool because they usually fly where the sun is bright. If you wish to decorate, keep bright colors to a minimum — thin pin stripes, identifying numbers, or perhaps a flag on the tail will suffice for most gliders.

NOTE: It is easier to partially cut out all the pieces first, leaving a small segment of each part attached. Then cut the remaining segments in turn, removing the parts from the card stock. This method of leaving the parts in place gives stability to the sheet while working.

A good work area for model building consists of a large flat surface for spreading things out and plenty of light to see what you are doing. Shown is the proper way to hold knife and paper.

HOW TO PROCEED

FIRST, make photocopies
Make *same-sized* photocopies (100%) of the pages containing the parts for building the paper gliders.

SECOND, prepare parts sheets
Cut the **parts layout section** from each photocopy, as indicated on the page, to fit a 5 x 8 inch standard index card. Then tack-glue to the card by applying glue to the areas *between* the parts (**on the backside**) aligning carefully with the edges of the card.

THIRD, advanced planning
Before beginning to cut out the parts, score those parts that will need to be bent later, and cut opening slits where indicated. Score and cut precisely on the lines.

FOURTH, cut out the parts
Cut out each part shown. This must be done carefully, since the success or failure of every other step depends on accurately made parts. *Keep track of the parts by lightly writing the part number in pencil on the backside of each part.*

FIFTH, build the fuselage
Begin with the number one fuselage part, adding the other smaller parts on each side to complete the fuselage. Align parts carefully. Add decoration when the glue is dry.

To camber the wings hold between thumb and forefinger of both hands, as shown. Working from the wing root to the wingtip, gently massage the paper to give the upper surface a convex curvature.

SIXTH, build the wings

Symmetry is essential for wings. Again, align parts carefully. Special care must be taken in those wings consisting of two halves. Temporarily align the halves using masking tape on the bottom side until the joining piece on the topside is glued in place. *The dihedral angle must be set before the glue has dried.* See the dihedral guide for details. Add decoration when the glue is dry.

SEVENTH, put it all together

Apply glue to the bent-over tabs that join the wings and horizontal stabilizer to the fuselage. Align the wings and stabilizers carefully. Press glued parts together. *Adjust placement carefully, viewing the glider from the top, the front, and the back.* **Symmetry and straight lines in the completed glider are essential.**

EIGHTH, camber the wings

This is a critical step . Cambering the wings gives them their ability to generate aerodynamic lift. Holding a wing at the root between thumb and forefinger of both hands, gently massage the paper to give the upper surface a slight convex curvature or camber. Work carefully from the wing root toward the tip and back again. Make sure the left and right wing have the same amount of camber. Avoid kinking the paper. See the instructions for each model for the proper amount of camber.

NINTH, test fly

This, too, is important. The paper glider must be well trimmed (adjusted) before it can perform satisfactorily. See page 93.

TENTH, fly for fun

Paper gliders perform best out-of-doors in a light breeze in wide-open spaces, away from obstructions and traffic.

Test flights, straight glides, and games such as flying through hoops and spot landings can be done satisfactorily indoors. Catching updrafts for soaring must be done in wide open spaces away from obstacles and traffic.

**Caution:
To avoid injury, never fly a paper glider toward another person.**

The Paperwing

This paper airplane is not modeled after any existing full-sized glider; rather, it is designed as a high perform-ance paper glider. It differs from the other examples in this book (and from full-sized gliders) in how its weight is distributed in relation to the lifting force of the wings. For improved performance, the center of gravity is located near the trailing (back) edge of the wings making the horizontal stabilizer act as a secondary wing. See pp 20-22 for a comparison with other aircraft. **(See text p 5.)**

Instructions

NOTE: Also refer to general instructions on pp 6-9.

1 See pages 12 and 13 for this step.

2 Tack-glue parts cutting guides onto index cards by gluing on the **back-side between the parts**.

3 Score the fold lines for wing and tail tabs. (After cutting out the pieces, bend tabs outward.)

4 Cut each piece from the index card stock. Remove light-weight guide paper and discard, leaving a clean unmarked glider part.

NOTE: Cut carefully through both sheets. The cutting side is always the upward or outward facing surface of the finished part.

NOTE: Ensure that the entire contacting surface of a smaller piece being fastened to a larger one is completely covered with glue.

4L
3L
2L
1F
2R
3R
4R

5 Glue pieces 1F through 4R and 4L to build up fuselage layers, carefully aligning parts.

Press fuselage flat between clean sheets of paper underneath a heavy weight (a few big books) until glue is sufficiently set (about 45 minutes).

6 Glue 6W to the bottom of wing part 5W.

5W

6W

9 Camber the wings by curving the paper gently between thumb and forefinger. See below.

7S

NOTE: Make sure wing parts are aligned along the centerline.

The dihedral angle of the wings must be set before the glue dries. See below.

7 Applying glue to the tail tabs, fasten horizontal stabilizer 10S to the fuselage.

8 Applying glue to the wing tabs, fasten wing assembly to the fuselage.

Camber:

point of maximum camber, 30% from front

correct

too much

Dihedral: 1 in (2.5 cm)

NOTE: After completing the glider, it is important to let the glue set completely (an hour or two) before flying.

The Paperwing

Parts

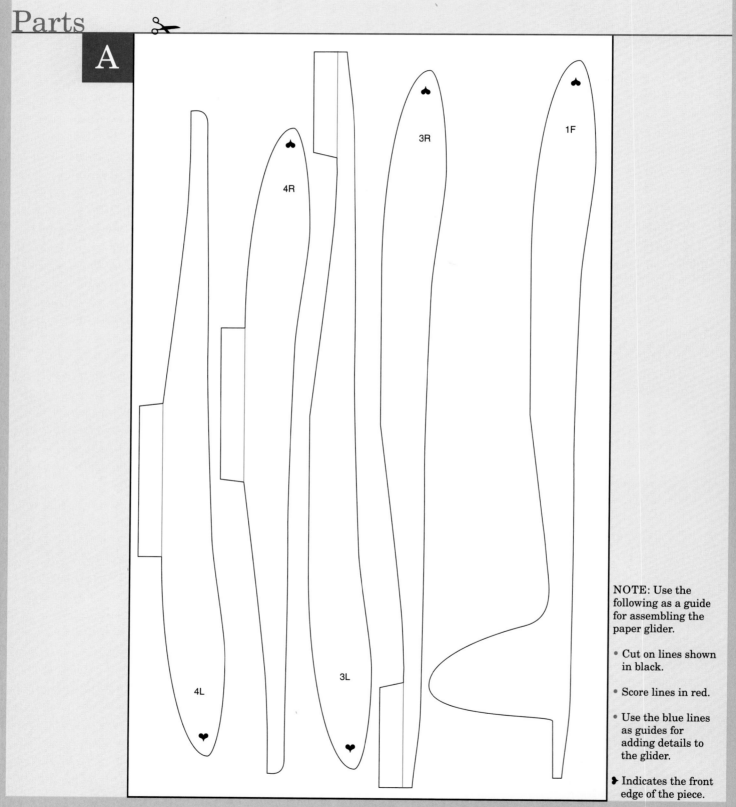

A

4R

3R

1F

4L

3L

NOTE: Use the following as a guide for assembling the paper glider.

- Cut on lines shown in black.

- Score lines in red.

- Use the blue lines as guides for adding details to the glider.

➤ Indicates the front edge of the piece.

First, photocopy these two pages (100% size). Do not cut the pages from the book .

Then cut out the portion indicated below from the photocopy.
This makes a cutting guide for the various parts and fits a
standard 5 x 8 inch index card. See page 11 for step two.

Parts

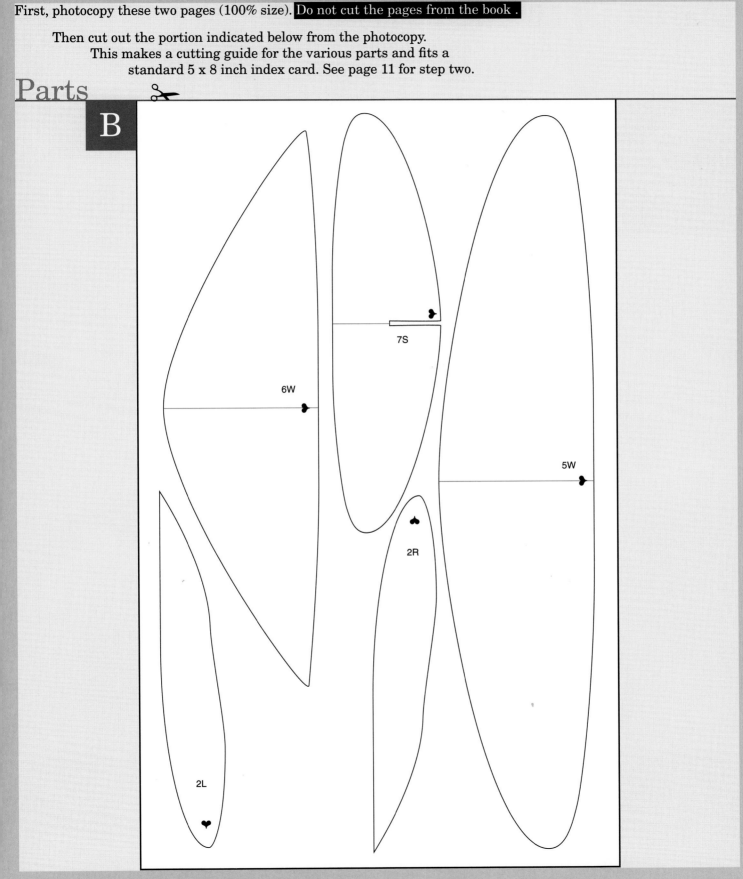

Glasflügel Libelle 201

This Standard Class sailplane, of German origin, was designed in 1964 by Eugen Hänle and Wolfgang Hütter. It is among the first all-fibreglass designs. On it pilots immediately set new records, and since then all high-perfomance sailplanes have been constructed of composite materials because of the better streamlining these materials allow. More than 700 Libelles are active worldwide, making it the most numerous model in that class. In 1969 it was voted the world's most beautiful sailplane. **(See text pp 5, 59, 60.)**

Instructions

NOTE: Also refer to general instructions on pp 6-9.

1 See pages 16 and 17 for this step.

2 Tack-glue parts cutting guides onto index cards by gluing on the **back-side between the parts**.

3 Cut opening in fuselage part for horizontal stabilizer.

5 Cut each piece from the index card stock. Remove lightweight guide paper and discard, leaving a clean unmarked glider part.

4 Score the fold lines for wing and tail tabs. (After cutting out the pieces, bend tabs outward.)

NOTE: Cut carefully through both sheets. The cutting side is always the upward or outward facing surface of the finished part.

6 Glue pieces 1F through 5R and 5L to build up fuselage layers, carefully aligning parts.

NOTE: Ensure that the entire contacting surface of a smaller piece being fastened to a larger one is completely covered with glue.

Press fuselage flat between clean sheets of paper underneath a heavy weight (a few big books) until glue is sufficiently set (about 45 minutes).

7 Bring wing parts 6R and 6L together, fastening with 7T. Then glue 8R and 8L to the bottom of the wing. Finally glue 9B to the very bottom.

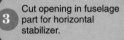

8 Applying glue to the tail tabs, fasten horizontal stabilizer 10S to the fuselage.

10 Camber the wings by curving the paper gently between thumb and forefinger. See below.

NOTE: Make sure wing parts are aligned along the centerline.

The dihedral angle of the wings must be set before the glue dries. See below.

9 Applying glue to the wing tabs, fasten wing assembly to the fuselage.

Camber:

point of maximum camber, 30% from front

correct

too much

Dihedral: 1 1/2 in (3.75 cm)

NOTE: After completing the glider, it is important to let the glue set completely (an hour or two) before flying.

Glasflügel Libelle 201

Parts

A

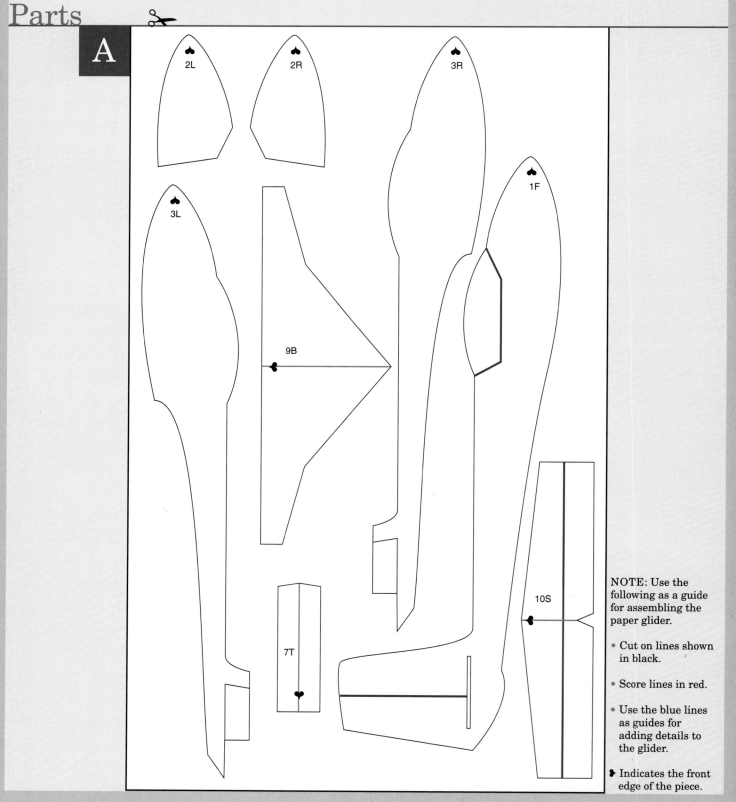

NOTE: Use the following as a guide for assembling the paper glider.

- Cut on lines shown in black.

- Score lines in red.

- Use the blue lines as guides for adding details to the glider.

➤ Indicates the front edge of the piece.

First, photocopy these two pages (100% size). Do not cut the pages from the book .

Then cut out the portion indicated below from the photocopy.
This makes a cutting guide for the various parts and fits a
standard 5 x 8 inch index card. See page 15 for step two.

Parts

B

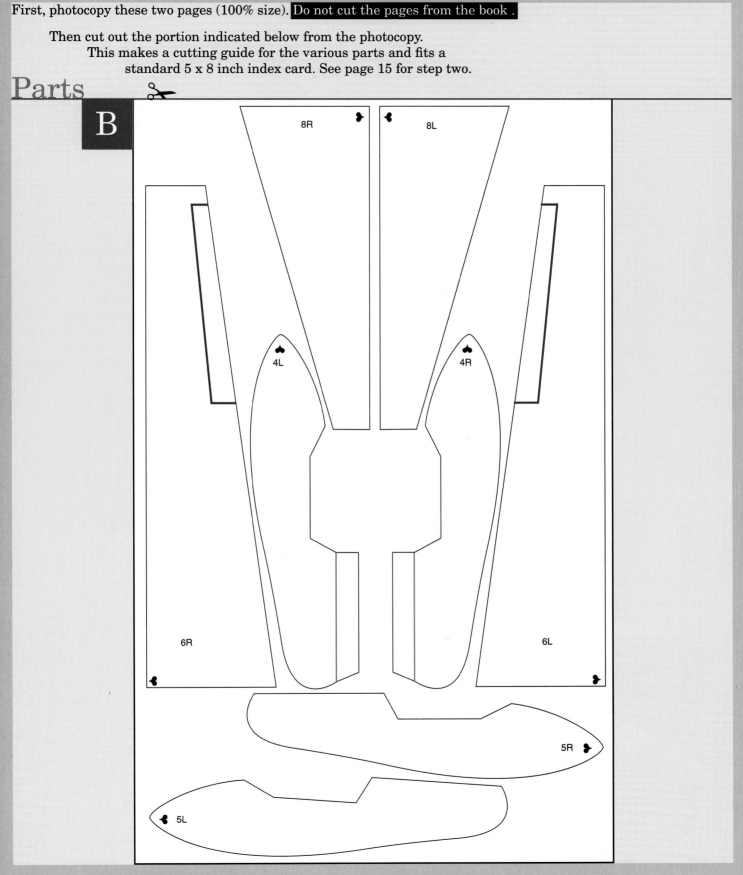

8R

8L

4L

4R

6R

6L

5R

5L

NVENTORS in ancient times, inspired by birds flying overhead, built the first flying machines — tethered kites. Free-flight was not so easily achieved. Since aerodynamic principles were unknown, the similarities between a kite flying on a string and a bird flying freely were not recognized. It was assumed that wing flapping was necessary to remain airborne. This idea was further reinforced by the fact that the similar action of rowing a boat in water worked very well. But had people paid more attention to hawks, eagles, and gulls, soaring overhead without so much as a single wingbeat, free-flight might have occurred much sooner than it did. It took many hundreds of years before anyone seriously looked to the soaring birds for clues.

In the 1500s Leonardo da Vinci made a modest beginning. He realized correctly that for successful flight it was the shape of the device flown that determined how the resisting force of moving air could be harnessed and controlled. However, even Leonardo did not understand that bird wings produce two independent forces — one for remaining airborne and the other for propulsion, and that flapping is involved only in the latter. Real progress did not occur for another 300 years when the basic principles of fluid dynamics were better understood; when in the mid-1700s, Swiss mathematician, Daniel Bernoulli, discovered that the pressure of a fluid always decreases as its rate of flow is increased (Bernoulli's Principle).

This law of nature explained that the same properties kept a bird, a kite, or an aircraft aloft. See figures 1 and 2.

In 1799 the Englishman, Sir George Cayley, experimenting with kites, was the first person to understand the separateness of the force of lift from thrust, and the application of aerodynamic principles. Cayley understood that controlling differential air pressure was the key to generating a lifting force and made careful studies of the ratio between wing shape and surface area to lifting capacity. He also undertood how the addition of smaller surfaces strategically located, gave stability. Cayley knew about the importance of adjusting surfaces to correct angles (called the angle of attack) relative to the airflow for balancing the various forces at play. He began by utilizing two arch top kites (a large one for producing lift and a smaller one for stability) combined into a single device.

Cayley was the first person to fly successfully many different kinds of small-scale wood and paper models. After 1806 he built machines with increasingly larger wing areas that could carry weights up to 80 or 90 pounds (36-41 kg). Cayley had replaced the smaller kite used for stability with a tail, introducing for the first time the concept of horizontal and vertical stabilizing surfaces. But these gliders could not be adjusted while in flight. They had to be trimmed for level flight before they were launched. Once airborne they could fly only straight ahead and were at the mercy of any fluctuations in air currents.

Figure 1

Demonstrating Bernoulli's Principle

Hold the narrow edge of a lightweight piece of writing paper (approximately 3 x 8 in or 7.5 x 20 cm) between thumb and forefinger, letting the free end droop. Then blow over your thumb and along the paper. If done correctly the drooping end should rise because the moving air exerts less pressure downward than the still air beneath does upward. Consequently the air beneath pushes the paper upward. A lifting force has been created.

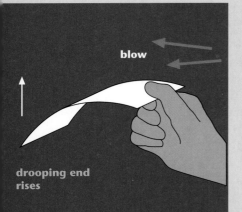

blow

drooping end rises

Figure 2

How a wing creates lift

A wing increases the speed of the airflow over its upper surface so that pressure in this area is reduced. This is accomplished by making the upper wing surface curved — called camber. The distance from front to back along the curved surface is greater than along the straight lower one. Because the molecules flowing along the curve have farther to travel than the ones beneath, they increase their speed and become spaced farther apart in order to resume their former position when they leave the wing at the trailing edge. This faster moving air exerts less pressure, which means that a partial vacuum is created above the wing — suction. (By the application of Bernoulli's Principle.) The now higher pressure beneath pushes the wing upward into the vacuum, creating a lifting force. This lift acts through a point about one third of the distance between the leading and trailing edges of a wing, the point of maximum camber.

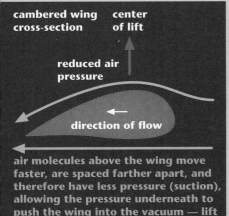

cambered wing   center
cross-section   of lift

reduced air
pressure

direction of flow

air molecules above the wing move faster, are spaced farther apart, and therefore have less pressure (suction), allowing the pressure underneath to push the wing into the vacuum — lift

Because of his many successful unmanned flights, in 1853 Cayley sent his coachman for a straight descending glide from a higher point to a lower one on his largest machine. It became the first observed and recorded occurrence of a human being in free-flight. For his work, Cayley earned the title of Father of Aviation. His work encouraged others to follow, but successful controlled flight eluded most of the early pioneers.

In Germany, however, Otto Lilienthal, a marine engineer, made real progress. After some twenty years of observing seagulls in flight and studying bird anatomy, in 1889 he published his *Der Vogel Flug als Grundlage der Fliegekunst* (Bird-flight as the basis for the Art of Flying).

For the first time someone was taking a new approach to the problems of flight by seriously studying birds, not for their wing flapping but for their gliding flight. The following year he built his first flying machine, modeled on his observations. Piloting — controlling the man-made "birds" while in flight — became one of his main objectives. He understood that the lifting force produced by the curvature of the feathers was improved by the fact that bird wings are longer than they are wide. Air resistance relative to the lifting force was less. Also, he saw that gulls make slight adjustments in the positions and angles of their wings and tails to balance themselves in gliding flight. Piloting therefore meant balancing the various forces at work as demanded by the fluctuations in air currents encountered while flying.

As a result of these observations the gliders he built assumed a bird-like shape, and the pilot moved his body about in flight to alter the relationship between the center of gravity and the lifting force of the wings. Lilienthal had invented the hang glider. **(Paper glider 3, p 28.)**

In the next five years Lilienthal made over 2000 successful gliding flights using weight shifting for balance, some covering distances of nearly 1000 feet (300 m). This method of maintaining equilibrium, however, has limitations. Rather than initiating guidance to the machine in a positive manner, weight shifting is always compensatory, the pilot reacting to the aircraft's movement in any direction. If a misjudgement is made in the position of the pilot's body, or unexpected gusts occur, the machine can become dangerously unstable. Weight shifting also limits the size of aircraft that can be successfully balanced to rather small and lightweight machines.

Unfortunately Lilienthal's calculations for wing size, lift, and air resistance were not very accurate. On August 9, 1896 his glider pitched up in a gust. He was unable to compensate by weight shifting and the craft stalled, pitched nose-down, and crashed. Lilienthal died from the injuries he sustained. But he had gained the reputation of being the first true pilot.

FLIGHT involves the creation of two forces by artificial means to oppose two forces occuring naturally — the force of lift must be created to counteract the earth's gravity, and the force of thrust to oppose air resistance.

GRAVITY AND LIFT

To work, aircraft wings must alter air pressure. They do this in two ways. First, as they move forward they slice the surrounding air into two layers, one above and one beneath the wings. Both layers are made up of the same number of molecules. If the wing has a curved upper surface, the molecules moving across the top surface have farther to travel than the ones underneath. As they try to maintain their position in relation to the rest of the air molecules, they become spaced farther apart and their speed increases so that when they reach the back edge of the wing, they again match their position with the lower molecules. In accordance with Bernoulli's Principle, the faster moving and more widely spaced molecules exert less pressure downward than the slower moving and more closely spaced lower molecules do upward, creating a pressure differential. The reduced pressure above the wings creates suction, much like a vacuum cleaner does. The air underneath pushes the wing into the area of reduced pressure, and the aircraft is buoyed up as it moves forward, counteracting gravity. (See figure 2, p 19).

Second, if the leading edge of the wings is raised slightly, allowing air molecules to strike the slanted lower surface, the amount of lift generated

can be increased. This slanting is called the *angle of attack*. See figure 3. However, if this angle is too great lift stops because air no longer flows smoothly over the upper surface disrupting the suction and the wing *stalls*. See figure 4.

DRAG AND THRUST

Lift is possible only by forward motion. As a glider moves forward air molecules are pushed aside causing a certain amount of resistance. On the one hand this resistance turns into the pressure that makes lift possible, on the other hand, it becomes drag, which slows a glider down. The resistance of air molecules being disturbed by forward motion is called *pressure drag*.

Figure 3
Increasing the lifting force

The lifting force created by a wing through reduced air pressure over the upper surface (suction) can be increased if the leading edge of the wing is raised slightly. This incline is called the angle of attack. It allows the airflow to strike the lower surface. As air is deflected downward, it provides a force in the opposite direction. This additional pressure beneath the wings increases the overall lifting force. Even a flat uncambered wing can generate lift just by having an angle of attack, as is the case in some kites. Over the years many different cambered wing shapes have been used on various aircraft. Powered aircraft that are designed to fly at very high speeds have thin wings with only slight camber. Glider wings have generous camber and are designed to produce the maximum amount of lift with a minimum penalty of drag at moderate speeds. Every wing design of any particular cross-section shape has a best angle of attack.

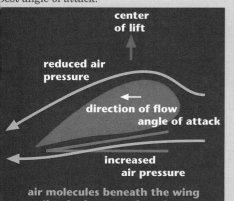

air molecules beneath the wing strike the lower surface, increasing the lifting force

Figure 4
Stall — if the angle of attack is too great the wing no longer produces lift

Lift stops if the angle of attack exceeds about 15 degrees because the air flowing over the upper surface, unable to follow the steep curve, separates and breaks into eddies. Then the air striking the lower surface creates a backward instead of upward force (drag).

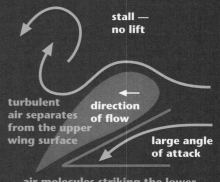

air molecules striking the lower surface create a backward instead of upward force

Figure 5

Drag — the resisting force of air
Thrust — a propelling force

Once launched, the force of gravity propels a glider through the air. This is called thrust. The steeper a plane's gliding angle the greater this force becomes, making the glider fly faster. But air resists being disturbed. This is called drag. It slows a glider down and its force increases with speed. Drag and thrust counteract each other.

There are three kinds of drag: pressure drag, induced drag, and frictional drag. These combine to make up the overall drag acting on an aircraft in flight. Pressure drag is the general resistance of air to disturbance. This is what you feel when you wave your arm or run. The bigger the frontal area of an object, the greater this drag. Air always flows from an area of high pressure to an area of low pressure: therefore, in the process of generating lift, air slips around the wingtips creating a vortex. This is induced drag. Because of the relative stickiness of air, any surface of the aircraft over which air flows creates frictional drag.

Excessive drag is the bane of gliders, and reducing it has been a major objective in sailplane design.

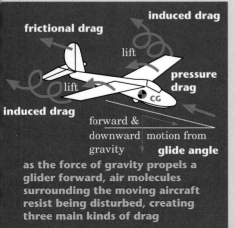

induced drag
frictional drag
lift
lift
pressure drag
induced drag
CG
forward & downward motion from gravity
glide angle

as the force of gravity propels a glider forward, air molecules surrounding the moving aircraft resist being disturbed, creating three main kinds of drag

This drag increases as a glider's speed increases. Furthermore, any surfaces on an airplane not parallel to the airflow add to this drag, including a wing's angle of attack and stabilizers adjusted to maintain straight and level flight.

Additionally, the pressure differential above and beneath a wing creates a vortex as air slips around the wingtip from the area of high pressure to that of low pressure. This turbulence, which always accompanies lift production, is called *induced drag*.

Air molecules flowing over an object also tend to stick to the object's surface, adding to the air's resistance — called *frictional drag*. The smaller the object and the slower it moves the greater the frictional drag. In fact, for a small flying insect, the air seems as thick and gooey as swimming in syrup would be to us.

The various types of drag combine into a single force as the glider moves forward through the air.

The presence of drag demands that a glider have a constant thrusting force to remain in motion. This is obtained by designing the glider so that the center of gravity (CG) — the point where the glider's weight appears to be concentrated — is slightly ahead of the point where the lifting force of the wings buoys up the glider (the center of lift). Because the glider's weight is thus concentrated in its nose, the force of gravity automatically moves the glider in both a forward and downward direction. See figure 5.

BALANCE AND STABILITY

The degree of stability inherent in an aircraft depends on its overall design. As Lilienthal had discovered, all aircraft in flight tend to be unstable in three ways: they roll left or right along a longitudinal axis, pitch nose up or down along a lateral axis running through the wings, and yaw from side to side around a vertical axis. The axes

Figure 6

Dihedral angle

The wings on most aircraft angle upward away from the fuselage. This gives roll stability. In level flight each wing produces the same amount of lift. When an aircraft with dihedral is banked, as when upset by a gust of wind, the downgoing wing's exposed surface lengthens and its lift consequently increases, while the upgoing wing's exposed area shortens and its lift decreases. This lift differential causes an opposite rolling force and the plane rights itself, restoring equilibrium. The greater the dihedral angle the more stable the airplane.

Paper gliders require a dihedral angle somewhat greater than full sized planes because their very light weight makes them susceptible to upset by even light gusts of wind.

equal lift on each side in level flight

unequal lift when upset

larger exposed wing area increases lift, righting the airplane

Figure 7

Three-axis control in a standard aircraft

An aircraft in flight can rotate about its center of gravity along three axes. (1) Its rolling motion is controlled by ailerons in the wings. (2) Pitch is controlled by an elevator in the horizontal stabilizer. (3) Yaw is controlled by a rudder in the vertical stabilizer. These are small flaps on the trailing edges that swing back and forth like a door on its hinges. When operated in harmony, these controls provide equilibrium in flight — three-axis control.

The ailerons move differentially, when one is moved up the other goes down, and vice versa, creating a difference in lift between the two wings — down, and lift is increased; up, and it is decreased. This makes the aircraft bank and turn to left or right.

By moving up or down, the elevator contols the air flowing over the horizontal stabilizer. When it is raised the pressure over the upper surface of the stabilizer increases, pushing downward, which pitches the nose up as the plane rotates about the center of gravity.

The rudder swings to left or right and keeps the aircraft pointing straight into the airflow during flight.

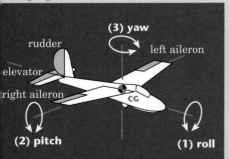

while in flight, the elevator, ailerons, and rudder allow for equilibrium to be maintained, as well as giving directional control for maneuvering the aircraft

intersect at the center of gravity. This means that an aircraft pivots freely about its center of gravity, and this movement must be stabilized for steady flight. Since Cayley's day it has been known that this can be accomplished by having both vertical and horizontal stabilizers and wings that slant upward slightly away from the fuselage (a dihedral angle). See figure 6.

Any upset by a gust of wind or turbulent air needs to be immediately corrected if steady flight is to be maintained. Therefore, besides having horizontal and vertical stabilizing surfaces, small moveable surfaces are required so that the pilot can make immediate adjustments to maintain equilibrium. These control surfaces must be large enough to also provide directional control for maneuvering the aircraft. See figure 7.

Neither Cayley nor Lilienthal had discoverd how moveable control surfaces could be added because the mechanisms required are complicated.

GLIDER PERFORMANCE

A glider's loss of height as gravity pulls it downward and forward is called sink. Every glider has a particular *rate of sink* , measured in units per minute. The amount of sink in relation to a glider's forward movement, is known as the *glide ratio*. At a constant airspeed the ratio of the lifting force of the wings and the resistant force of drag is exactly equal to the glide ratio. Therefore for a glider to have a high glide ratio, drag must be kept at a minimum. See figure 8.

Dividing the weight of a glider by the surface area of its wings is a ratio known as *wing loading*. The lighter the wing loading the smaller the sink rate, and the longer a glider will remain aloft in still air. It "floats." Gliders with very light wing loadings have limited usefulness. They are at the mercy of turbulence. For operation in the varied conditions found in the atmosphere greater wing loadings are needed to give higher airspeed and greater stability in rough air. This discovery in the 1920s was a major advance in soaring. Because of their light weight, paper gliders are all "floaters," especially the first model in this book, which is of non-conventional configuration.

Proper elevator adjustment is important to maximize performance in gliding flight. In aircraft of conventional configuration the horizontal stabilizer and the elevator provide a counterbalancing force compensating for the automatic downward pitching motion due to the center of gravity's location ahead of the center of lift. Furthermore, in all gliding flight, controlling pitch is especially important because it also controls airspeed. Airspeed, in turn, affects the glide ratio and overall performance of the glider. Every glider has an optimum speed for a best glide ratio. This is its cruising speed. Adjusting a glider to fly at this speed is called *trimming for cruise*. See figure 9.

Cayley and Lilienthal had only limited success in maintaining a plane's equilibrium. Their gliders were not maneuverable. For this a new design was needed.

Figure 8
Glider performance

If a glider produces a lot of drag in relation to the lifting force of its wings, it must descend rapidly to the ground in order for the force of gravity to maintain adequate forward momentum. It has a steep glide angle, and thus a poor glide ratio because it cannot travel very far before it lands. On the other hand, a glider producing little drag in relation to the lifting force of its wings flies with a shallower glide angle and can fly much farther. It has a high glide ratio. The relationship between the amount of lift that a wing produces and its accompanying drag at a particular speed is exactly the same ratio as that between a glider's height and its glide distance. That is, the lift to drag ratio and the glide ratio are identical.

If a wing has a lift to drag ratio of 30:1, that number is also the glider's glide ratio. In practical terms it means that for roughly every 5000 feet of altitude it can travel thirty miles.

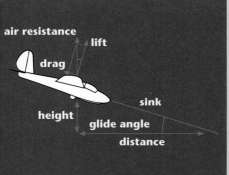

the lift to drag ratio and the glide ratio (height to distance) are identical

ILIENTHAL'S records became the basis for the work of Wilbur and Orville Wright, two American bicycle builders who turned their attention to airplanes. They began their work with the newly-invented box kite. They made detailed observations of aerodynamic properties and applied new findings carefully. To aid in their work they constructed a wind tunnel in which conditions could be controlled for observation. In it they tested small models.

Their full-sized models were tested at Kitty Hawk, in North Carolina. First they made tethered flights, then proceeded to free-flight, and by the end of 1900, they had made their first successful manned gliding flights.

On their machines the pilot worked hand and foot operated moveable surfaces to achieve stability in three axes — the wingtips were differentially twisted to control roll, the elevator in the horizontal stabilizer controlled pitch, and the rudder in the tail controlled yaw. This gave them sufficient control to maintain stability in rough as well as smooth air, and provided directional control for maneuvering the glider.

Three-axis control was the Wright brothers' first and greatest contribution to aeronautics. It has become standardized, with variations, in all aircraft except hang gliders, where weight shifting is still utilized. See figure 7.

The Wrights next addressed regular sustained flight. For this they would need a means of propulsion. Steam engines had been tried but were too heavy. The Wright brothers recognized the potential of Gottlieb Daimler and Karl Benz's gasoline burning internal combustion engine, and set about designing a small lightweight version of their own. When fitted to their airplane it

Figure 9
Performance and speed

In motorless aircraft, airspeed is controlled solely by altering pitch. This is done by adjusting the elevator. In a glider of ordinary design the center of gravity is located ahead of the center of lift. This configuration allows a slightly raised elevator (positive trim) to pitch the nose up a little, causing the glider to fly with a particular angle of attack. Increase the pitch and the glider flies at a slower speed. Decrease it and speed increases.

Every wing is most efficient at a particular angle of attack and speed. This speed must be maintained for a best glide ratio. Therefore a certain amount of positive trim is always necessary to maintain a proper flight attitude. Positive trim also helps in maintaining balance despite any air turbulence. Gliders that have a best glide ratio at higher speeds are better able to penetrate rough air.

Given the comparative lightness of gliders, the location of the CG relative to the center of lift is critical for correctly counterbalancing weight (acting through the CG) by elevator trim to achieve good performance. In most gliders the speed range for maximum performance is quite narrow.

with elevator raised, airflow is deflected upward, increasing pressure above the horizontal stabilizer

lift

CG

the tail is pushed downward and the nose pitches up

weight
CG ahead of lift

the location of the center of gravity, relative to the wing's lift, is important for proper pitch trim and good glide performance proved to have just the right ratio of power to weight to get the craft off the ground. Thus in 1903 the era of powered flight began. The thrusting force that the wing flapping of birds provides was successfully emulated by the spinning propeller. This is the second contribution the Wrights made to aviation.

In 1911 Orville Wright returned to Kitty Hawk for further experiments to learn something about soaring flight and to take advantage of the rising air currents and remain aloft without an artificial source of power. Orville was accompanied by Alec Ogilvie, a fellow aviation pioneer from Britain. They modified the Wright glider no. 5 by lengthening the fuselage, adding a forward boom that carried a sandbag as ballast, and adding supplementary stabilizers. The success of their flights in this modified glider was remarkable. Orville describes the event:

In 1911 Mr. Alec Ogilvie and I continued the soaring experiments at Kitty Hawk and succeeded in making a number of flights of more than five minutes duration (the longest of which was nine and three-quarters minutes) without loss of any height at all. In many cases we landed at a higher point than the one from which we started. I see no reason why flights of several hours duration cannot be made without the use of a motor. But, of course, these flights must be made in rising trends of air — a condition required by all birds for soaring flight.

This event marked the first recorded human soaring flight. For the first time humans could do what the soaring birds did. This is the third contribution the Wrights made to aviation. Henceforth aircraft development would be along two distinct lines — powered and motorless.

Orville Wright soars the Wright Glider no. 5 over the sand dunes of Kitty Hawk, making the world's first sustained motorless flight.

O RVILLE'S success at soaring stimulated great enthusiasm and began a grassroots movement of gliding experiments. But the war in Europe in 1914, forced everyone involved in aviation to divert their attention from motorless flight to perfecting the powered airplane as a weapon of war.

When the war ended in 1918 Americans began to develop the powered airplane that had great military and commercial potential, which they rapidly exploited. Germany, which was forbidden by the Treaty of Versailles to develop aircraft for military use, turned to gliders. No powered aircraft could be built. Germany's engineers, scientists, and aviation enthusiasts pursued gliding flight with a passion, and it became an official technical subject in universities.

A magazine, *Flugsport* (Sport Aviation), emphasized the sporting potential of soaring flight, and widely popularized the activity. In 1919 the first soaring meet was held at the Wasserkuppe in the Rhoen mountain range of central Germany, an ideal site with smooth slopes for launching gliders as well as ridges for producing rising currents of air.

The next year, 1920, the meet became an official competition, setting the stage for what has come to characterize the world of soaring flight — achieving goals and setting records. This first official soaring competition produced a winning flight of 2 minutes 23 seconds, achieved by Wolfgang Klemperer.

In the 1921 meet, Klemperer made some significant improvements to his glider and achieved a 13 minute flight. Orville's record had fallen.

For this meet, for the first time, a system of "A" "B" and "C" achievement badges was established, and Klemperer's was the first "C" badge given. ("C" designated a flight of 5 minutes duration. The "A" and "B" badges were given for piloting proficiency.)

The next day, a student named Martens, broke Klemperer's record with a 15 minute flight, and later another student, named Harth, made a 21 minute flight, more than doubling Orville's time. He achieved the third "C" badge in the world.

This systematic marking of soaring achievements is still in place today, and all soaring pilots participate in it. The "A" badge now designates solo flight, "B" the first solo soaring flight, "C" one hour of soaring flight, and so on, including not only duration but also distances covered, speeds attained, altitudes gained, and various combinations of achievements in "silver," "gold," and "diamond" catagories.

In 1922 national meets were also held in Britain and France, beginning a trend that continues to this day, when many countries around the world hold annual national soaring competitions.

In England, a French pilot named Manyrolle raised the record time considerably with a flight of 3 hours 20 minutes. Orville's prediction of prolonged motorless flight had been realized.

Gliders of every description were being built. According to a U.S. pilot and military observer named Allen, the gliders of the day could be put into four classes of machines: (1) sailplanes, gliders with improved performance, (2) hang gliders, primitive machines having weight-shifting control, (3) powerplanes with engines removed, and (4) freaks of all kinds, built by non-technical enthusiasts.

Gliders were launched down a slope using an elastic shock cord. Either a number of people or horses were used to stretch the cord while the glider was held fast. Once the cord was fully extended the glider was released and catapulted into the air.

At that time the goal of soaring was duration flying. The source of lift was the band of air forced upward as wind strikes rising ground called *ridge lift*, which the Wrights had also used. Because the gliders didn't go anywhere, most designers concentrated on the lightness of their craft, slow air speed, and a low sink rate, which they thought would keep them aloft the longest. See figure 10.

German designers had other ideas. They built sailplanes that were heavier with higher wing loadings, had increased air speeds, higher aspect ratios with greater lift-to-drag ratios, making them less susceptible to upsets in gusty conditions and better able to penetrate rough air. In such machines pilots could venture outside the sources of lift and fly from place to place away from the ridges.

Through consistent and organized effort, after the first world war, they had moved far ahead of the rest of the world in several ways: developing the performance levels of sail-planes, gaining an understanding of meteorological conditions, and refining soaring techniques to suit different conditions.

In the United States at this time most aviation remained largely a military affair. But it was brought sharply into the American public mind in 1927 when Charles Lindbergh made his dramatic trans-Atlantic solo flight. North Americans became "air minded."

Popular scientific magazines advertised blueprints, of German origin, that could be ordered for the home building of primary gliders. These consisted of open-frame fuselages with the pilot seated unenclosed in the nose, with wings and stabilizers supported by wire braces. They made aviation available to an eager public. **(Paper glider 4, p 32.)**

Meanwhile, Wasserkuppe had become a soaring mecca for testing new designs and flight duration challenges. Schools were established in Germany and other parts of Europe and the U.S. for proper flight training. A gliding school was established in 1928 at Cape Cod, Massachusetts, where Ralph Barnaby achieved the first American "C" badge with a flight of 15 minutes. Soon thereafter Peter Hesselbach, the school's chief pilot, set an American record with a flight of over 4 hours.

In 1929 Hawley Bowlus in the U.S. built a high-performance sailplane, known as the *Paperwing*. It was so named because ordinary butcher

Figure 10

Soaring flight in ridge lift

When wind blows against ground that is rising, air is deflected upward. Gliders can fly back and forth in this band of rising air along the crest of the ridge and remain airborne as long as this air is rising as fast as or faster than the glider's sink rate.

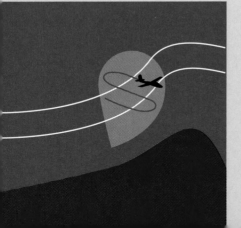

paper was used in its construction. In this plane he pushed the American soaring record to almost 9 hours. But most American gliding flights at that time, were measured, not even in minutes, but in seconds.

More enthusiasm for gliding in the U.S. occurred during the depression which began in 1929. Dwindling resources forced many aviation enthusiasts to give up powered flight. To remain active in aviation they turned to gliding, which was less costly. And as sales of powered aircraft decreased, established airplane manufacturers turned to building primary gliders, which they sold at very low cost. As a result, for the first time, factory built gliders were widely available in the U.S.

In 1928 Edward Evans, financier and director of the Aviation Bureau of the Detroit Board of Commerce, began a gliding club. Before long this club's mandate was broadened to become the National Glider Association, encouraging many other clubs to form. But the pilots remained largely untrained and there were many crashes.

In 1930 Elmira, New York was chosen by the NGA for the first American National glider meet. It was ideal for generating updrafts in wind blowing in almost any direction, and the valleys below had many ideal landing fields. On the very first flight there, Jack O'Meara logged 1 hour 34 minutes. With this site, soaring in the United States became solidly established. The National Soaring Museum is located there.

NATIONAL SOARING MUSEUM

Charles Lindbergh preparing for launch in a Bowlus Paperwing, 1930.

Lilienthal 1895 Glider

3

Otto Lilienthal observed birds in flight and studied their anatomy before he built his first glider in 1890. His bird-like machine was a hang glider, on which the pilot hung from a harness inside a hoop and shifted his weight — forward and backward or side to side — to maintain flight equilibrium. Over the next few years he built various models of hang gliders, some of which were biplanes. **(See text p 19.)**

Instructions

NOTE: Also refer to general instructions on pp 6-9.

1 See pages 30 and 31 for this step.

2 Tack-glue parts cutting guides onto index cards by gluing on the **back-side between the parts**.

3 Cut openings in fuselage and wings for horizontal stabilizer and pilot.

4 Score the fold lines for wing and tail tabs. (After cutting out the pieces, bend tabs outward.)

5 Cut each piece from the index card stock. Remove lightweight guide paper and discard, leaving a clean unmarked glider part.

NOTE: Cut carefully through both sheets. The cutting side is always the upward or outward facing surface of the finished part.

6 Glue pieces 1F through 9R and 9L to build up fuselage layers, carefully aligning parts.

NOTE: Ensure that the entire contacting surface of a smaller piece being fastened to a larger one is completely covered with glue.

Press fuselage flat between clean sheets of paper underneath a heavy weight (a few big books) until glue is sufficiently set (about 45 minutes).

7 Glue 11B to the bottom of wing part 10W.

10W

11B

NOTE: Make sure wing parts are aligned along the centerline.

The dihedral angle of the wings must be set before the glue dries. See below.

8 Applying glue to the tail tabs, fasten horizontal stabilizer 12S to the fuselage.

12S

9 Applying glue to the wing tabs, fasten wing assembly to the fuselage. Pilot goes through wing slot.

10 Camber the wings by curving the paper gently between thumb and forefinger. See below.

point of maximum camber, 30% from front

Camber:

correct

too much

1/2 in (1.25 cm)

NOTE: After completing the glider, it is important to let the glue set completely (an hour or two) before flying.

1F 2L 3L 4L 5L 6L 7L 8L 9L

2R 3R 4R 5R 6R 7R 8R 9R

Lilienthal 1895 Glider

Parts

A

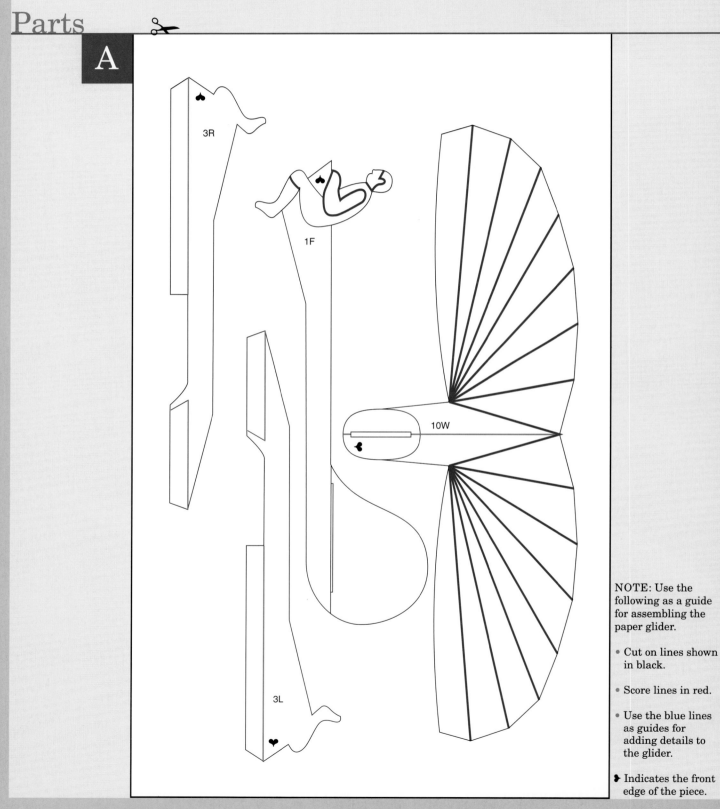

NOTE: Use the following as a guide for assembling the paper glider.

- Cut on lines shown in black.

- Score lines in red.

- Use the blue lines as guides for adding details to the glider.

❧ Indicates the front edge of the piece.

First, photocopy these two pages (100% size). Do not cut the pages from the book .

Then cut out the portion indicated below from the photocopy.
This makes a cutting guide for the various parts and fits a
standard 5 x 8 inch index card. See page 29 for step two.

Parts

B

6L

6R

9R

9L

4L

4R

11B

5L

5R

12S

7L

7R

2R

8L

2L

8R

Primary Glider

4

In the 1930s mail order blueprints for home building open-framed gliders — called primary gliders — having wire-braced fabric-covered wings and stabilizers, were advertised extensively in popular scientific magazines. Anyone handy with basic tools could build one in the home workshop. Later they were also factory built. These primitive machines played an important role in introducing gliding to the public. **(See text p 26.)**

Instructions

NOTE: Also refer to general instructions on pp 6-9.

1 See pages 34 and 35 for this step.

2 Tack-glue parts cutting guides onto index cards by gluing on the **back-side between the parts**.

4 Cut each piece from the index card stock. Remove light-weight guide paper and discard, leaving a clean unmarked glider part.

3 Score the fold lines for wing and tail tabs. (After cutting out the pieces, bend tabs outward.)

NOTE: Cut carefully through both sheets. The cutting side is always the upward or outward facing surface of the finished part.

9L 8L 7L 6L 5L 4L 3L 2L 1F 1F 2R 3R 4R 5R 6R 7R 8R 9R

5 Glue pieces 1F through 9R and 9L to build up fuselage layers, carefully aligning parts.

NOTE: Ensure that the entire contacting surface of a smaller piece being fastened to a larger one is completely covered with glue.

Press fuselage flat between clean sheets of paper underneath a heavy weight (a few big books) until glue is sufficiently set (about 45 minutes).

6 Glue 11B to the bottom of wing part 10W.

10W

11B

7 Applying glue to the tail tabs, fasten horizontal stabilizer 12S to the fuselage.

9 Camber the wings by curving the paper gently between thumb and forefinger. See below.

12S

NOTE: Make sure wing parts are aligned along the centerline.

The dihedral angle of the wings must be set before the glue dries. See below.

8 Applying glue to the wing tabs, fasten wing assembly to the fuselage.

Camber:

point of maximum camber, 30% from front

correct

too much

Dihedral: $^1/_2$ in (1.25 cm)

NOTE: After completing the glider, it is important to let the glue set completely (an hour or two) before flying.

Primary Glider

Parts

A

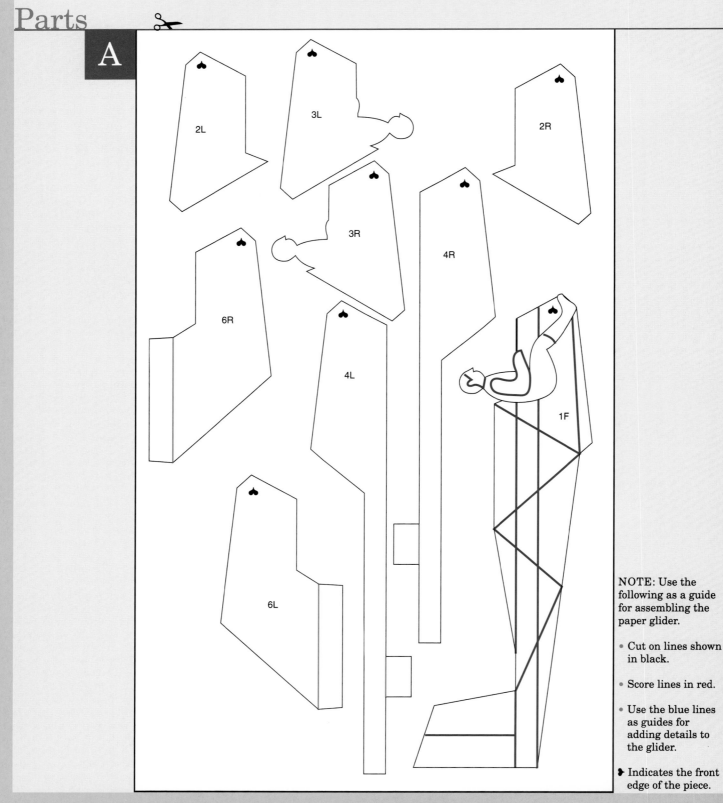

NOTE: Use the following as a guide for assembling the paper glider.

- Cut on lines shown in black.
- Score lines in red.
- Use the blue lines as guides for adding details to the glider.
- ➤ Indicates the front edge of the piece.

First, photocopy these two pages (100% size). Do not cut the pages from the book .

Then cut out the portion indicated below from the photocopy.
This makes a cutting guide for the various parts and fits a
standard 5 x 8 inch index card. See page 33 for step two.

Parts

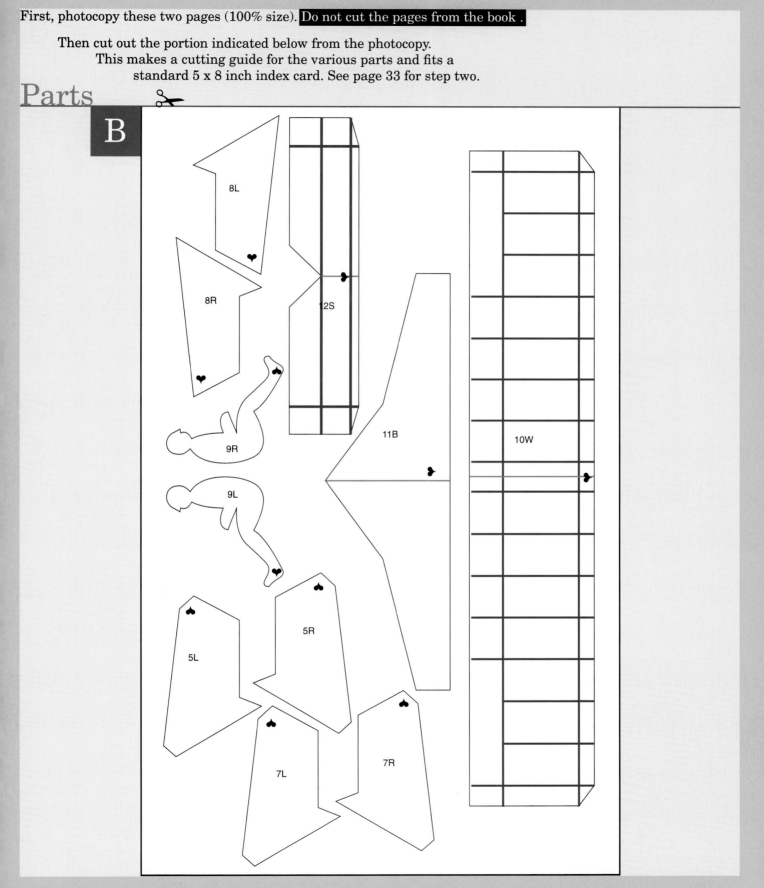

W HEN the first American national meet was held in 1930 meterological conditions necessary for soaring were just beginning to be understood by glider pilots. Largely unknown to American pilots was the fact that sustained flight was possible not only in ridge lift, but also over flatland warmed by the sun, in *thermal lift*. American pilots had sometimes encountered such lift away from the ridges, but flew right through it, not realizing that this lift ran in a vertical direction. The Germans, on the other hand, already knew how to use thermal lift but kept it a secret to maintain a competitive edge. German pilot Wolf Hirth used thermals to fly away from the ridges for a distance of 33 miles. His was the best flight of the meet. He was one of the top soaring pilots in the world at the time. Some time later he admitted that he had a "secret" instrument whereby areas of rising air could be determined. See figure 11.

Soon all glider pilots were no longer interested only in duration, but also in distances covered, speed, and altitudes gained. As the glide performance and flight characteristics of sailplanes improved, pilots became bolder in flying from one source of lift to another. Now thermal lift, which can be found anywhere, has surpassed ridge lift as the primary means of staying aloft in a sailplane because it gives the pilot freedom. And Hirth's "secret" instrument, the variometer, a sensitive rate-of-climb indicator, has become the soaring pilot's most important instrument.

By 1932 the NGA had been replaced by the Soaring Society of America, reflecting the shift in emphasis from gliding flight to soaring flight.

The SSA continued to hold national meets, and at the fifth American national meet in 1934 the distance record was pushed to 158 miles, and for the first time it was set by an American pilot, flying an American designed and built sailplane. But a month later at the 15th Wasserkuppe meet four German pilots exeeded the record, with Wolf Hirth in the lead having flown 218 miles. Altitudes in excess of 6000 feet, using thermal lift, were also attained. The Germans had developed the tight-turn spiraling technique of thermal soaring.

This technique was demonstrated to Americans for the first time at the 1937 American meet by German pilot, Peter Riedel. It has today become part of the standard training syllabus. That year also saw, for the first time, the aerotowing technique of launching used for competition sailplanes. It is now the standard launch method. In 1938 two-place training gliders were introduced to the U.S. For the first time it put the flight instructor into the cockpit with the student pilot, eliminating the need for instructions from the ground by hand signals and shouting.

World records kept climbing, and in 1938 the distance record was held by the Russians with 405 miles. An altitude of 14,189 feet had been attained by the Germans. American pilots realized the importance of location to record setting and used sites over the deserts where

Figure 11
Soaring flight in thermal lift

On a sunny day the earth is warmed by the sun's rays. This heat is radiated into the air which then becomes warmed. The warm air, being lighter, begins to form a bubble. It eventually breaks free, rises, and joins other bubbles becoming a column called a thermal. A glider circling inside this column can remain airborne as long as the air is rising as fast as or faster than the glider's sink rate. It can climb to the very top of the thermal, which is sometimes 10,000 feet (3000 m) or more in height. At the top of a thermal a cumulus cloud is often formed because the moist warm air from the ground rises into cold air aloft and the moisture condenses into a cloud. These clouds are important clues for glider pilots about where to find the next source of lift.

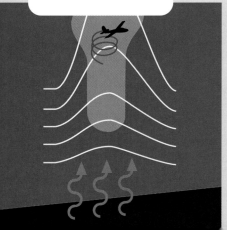

thermals were strong to achieve heights in excess of 10,000 feet (3000 m).

As in many parts of the world, Canadian soaring did not really get going until after the second world war. Before that time it was a disorganized effort: at best with local clubs setting their own standards and rules, at worst with individual "daredevils" building primary gliders in their backyards. But in 1939 Evelyn Fletcher, of the Lethbridge Gliding Club, flew a German Hütter H-17, for a distance of 10 miles, attaining an altitude of 4000 feet in a flight lasting 51 minutes, setting a Canadian record that was to stand for 10 years. In the meantime, in 1944, the Soaring Association of Canada was formed to promote and organize motorless flight across the country.

By the end of the 1930s plans had been laid to make gliding an Olympic Event. This would have been a tremendous boost to the sport. But it was not to be. In the fall of 1939 Germany invaded Poland engulfing the world in war, and suspending the Games. Several designs had already been submitted as possible Olympic Sailplanes. One was the Orlik designed by H. Kocjan of Poland. **(Paper glider 5, p 38.)**

In 1938 the ninth American national soaring meet was won by Emil Lehecka flying a high performance German-built Rhoensperber glider.

5

This glider was designed in Poland in the late 1930s for competition in the Olympic Games. It had an all-wood structure with fabric covering. Due to the war, the Olympic Games of 1940 were not held. In 1948, when the Games resumed, gliding was not among the events scheduled. However, the plane was used for other competitions. **(See text p 37.)**

Instructions

NOTE: Also refer to general instructions on pp 6-9.

1 See pages 40 and 41 for this step.

2 Tack-glue parts cutting guides onto index cards by gluing on the **back-side between the parts**.

3 Score the fold lines for wing and tail tabs. (After cutting out the pieces, bend tabs outward.)

4 Cut each piece from the index card stock. Remove light-weight guide paper and discard, leaving a clean unmarked glider part.

NOTE: Cut carefully through both sheets. The cutting side is always the upward or outward facing surface of the finished part.

5 Glue pieces 1F through 8R and 8L to build up fuselage layers, carefully aligning parts.

NOTE: Ensure that the entire contacting surface of a smaller piece being fastened to a larger one is completely covered with glue.

Press fuselage flat between clean sheets of paper underneath a heavy weight (a few big books) until glue is sufficiently set (about 45 minutes).

6 Bring wing parts 9R and 9L together, fastening with 10T. Then glue 11R and 11L to the bottom of the wing. Finally glue 12B to the very bottom.

7 Applying glue to the tail tabs, fasten horizontal stabilizer 13S to the fuselage.

9 Camber the wings by curving the paper gently between thumb and forefinger. See below.

NOTE: Make sure wing parts are aligned along the centerline.

The dihedral angle of the wings must be set before the glue dries. See below.

8 Applying glue to the wing tabs, fasten wing assembly to the fuselage.

point of maximum camber, 30% from front

Camber:

correct

too much

Dihedral: 1 1/2 in (3.75 cm)

NOTE: After completing the glider, it is important to let the glue set completely (an hour or two) before flying.

8L 7L 6L 5L 1F 2L 3L 4L 2R 3R 4R 5R 6R 7R 8R

9L 10T 11L 9R 11R 12B 13S

Orlik

Parts

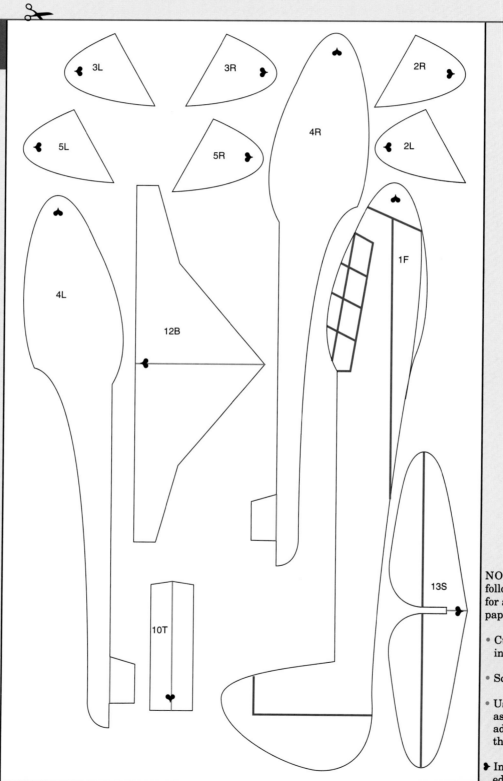

A

3L

3R

2R

4R

2L

5L

5R

1F

4L

12B

13S

10T

NOTE: Use the following as a guide for assembling the paper glider.

- Cut on lines shown in black.

- Score lines in red.

- Use the blue lines as guides for adding details to the glider.

⟩ Indicates the front edge of the piece.

First, photocopy these two pages (100% size).

Then cut out the portion indicated below from the photocopy.
This makes a cutting guide for the various parts and fits a
standard 5 x 8 inch index card. See page 39 for step two.

Parts

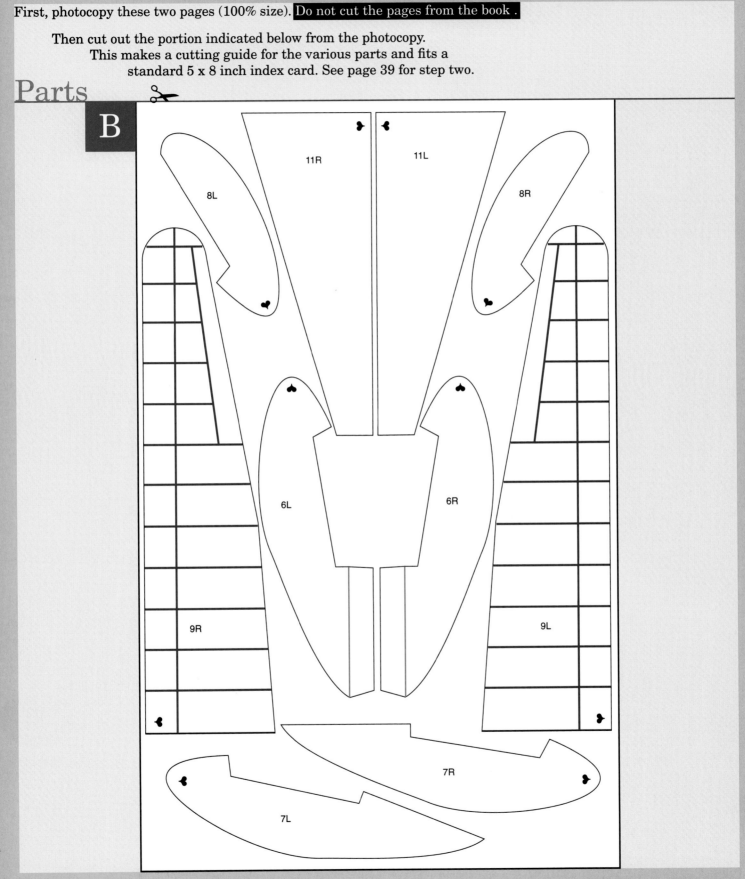

Grunau Baby

6

The Grunau Baby, designed in Germany in 1928, is a simple all-wood framed and fabric covered glider of modest performance. It originally had a simple skid landing gear (no wheel). This little glider became very popular in Europe and elsewhere, with many thousands being built around the world over a period of years. **(See text p 56.)**

Instructions

NOTE: Also refer to general instructions on pp 6-9.

1 See pages 44 and 45 for this step.

2 Tack-glue parts cutting guides onto index cards by gluing on the **back-side between the parts**.

3 Score the fold lines for wing and tail tabs. (After cutting out the pieces, bend tabs outward.)

4 Cut each piece from the index card stock. Remove light-weight guide paper and discard, leaving a clean unmarked glider part.

NOTE: Cut carefully through both sheets. The cutting side is always the upward or outward facing surface of the finished part.

5 Glue pieces 1F through 7R and 7L to build up fuselage layers, carefully aligning parts.

7L, 6L, 5L, 4L, 3L, 2L, 1F, 2R, 3R, 4R, 5R, 6R, 7R

NOTE: Ensure that the entire contacting surface of a smaller piece being fastened to a larger one is completely covered with glue.

Press fuselage flat between clean sheets of paper underneath a heavy weight (a few big books) until glue is sufficiently set (about 45 minutes).

6 Glue 9M to the bottom of wing part 8W. Then glue 10B to the bottom of 9M.

8W
9M
10B

NOTE: Make sure wing parts are aligned along the centerline.

The dihedral angle of the wings must be set before the glue dries. See below.

7 Applying glue to the tail tabs, fasten horizontal stabilizer 11S to the fuselage.

11S

9 Camber the wings by curving the paper gently between thumb and forefinger. See below.

8 Applying glue to the wing tabs, fasten wing assembly to the fuselage.

Camber:

point of maximum camber, 30% from front

correct

too much

Dihedral: $^3/_4$ in (2 cm)

NOTE: After completing the glider, it is important to let the glue set completely (an hour or two) before flying.

Grunau Baby

Parts

A

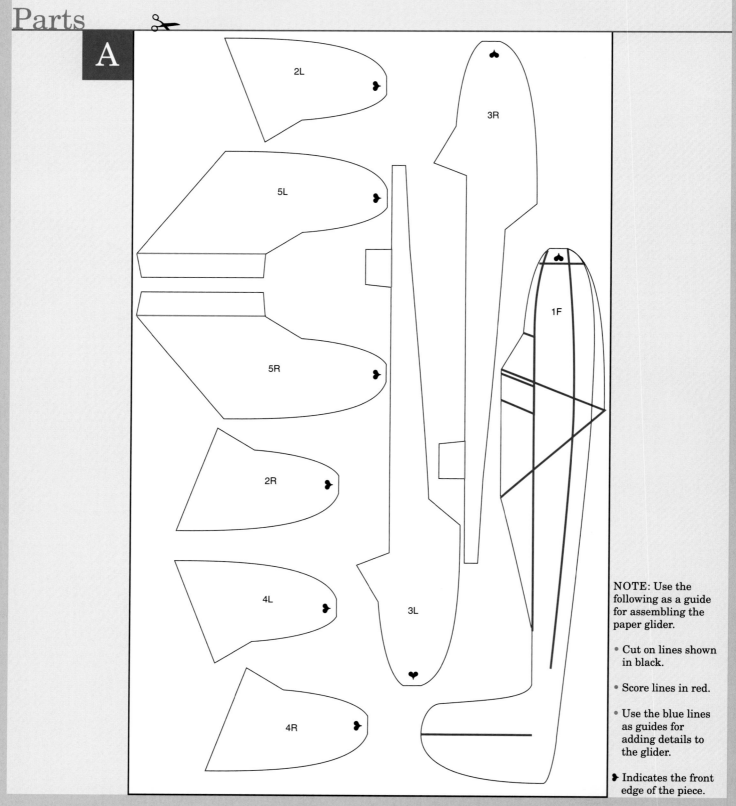

2L

3R

5L

1F

5R

2R

3L

4L

4R

NOTE: Use the following as a guide for assembling the paper glider.

• Cut on lines shown in black.

• Score lines in red.

• Use the blue lines as guides for adding details to the glider.

♣ Indicates the front edge of the piece.

First, photocopy these two pages (100% size). Do not cut the pages from the book .

Then cut out the portion indicated below from the photocopy.
This makes a cutting guide for the various parts and fits a
standard 5 x 8 inch index card. See page 43 for step two.

Parts

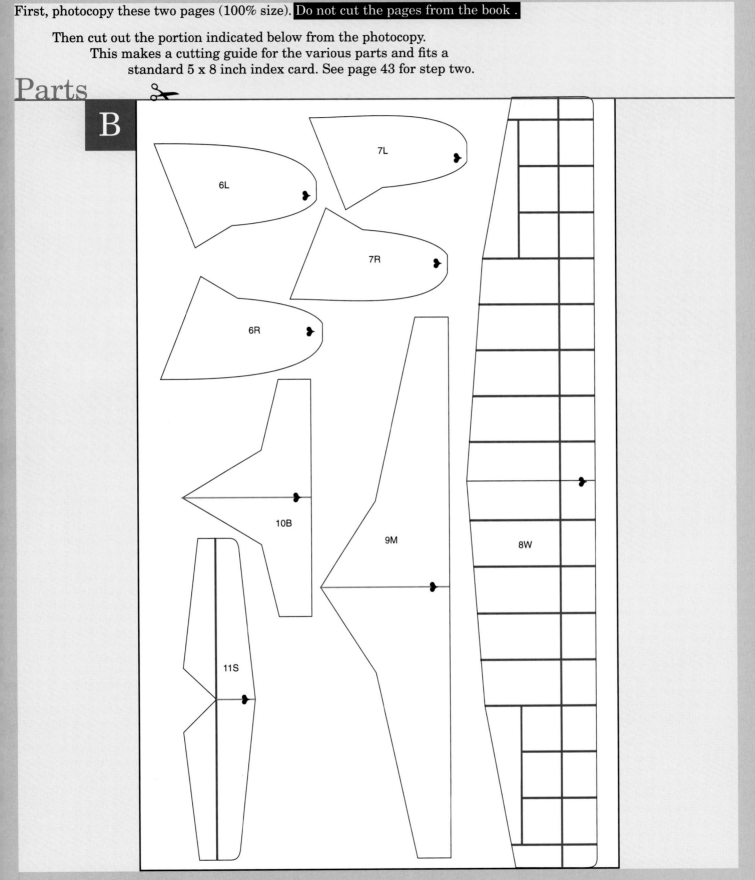

Waco CG-4

7

This glider was designed by the Waco Aircraft Company and built by various manufacturers across the U.S. in large numbers as a military transport plane. It could carry any combination of either 15 fully equiped troops, a small field gun, a jeep, or a loaded trailer. The gliders were towed, usually in pairs, behind a powered transport aircraft such as the C-47 Dakota (which in civilian service was the Douglas DC-3). Once released they were a stealthy aircraft that could deliver troops and equipment behind enemy lines. The entire nose section, including the cockpit, tilted up, allowing for cargo access. **(See text p 56.)**

Instructions

NOTE: Also refer to general instructions on pp 6-9.

1 See pages 48 through 51 for this step.

2 Tack-glue parts cutting guides onto index cards by gluing on the **back-side between the parts**.

3 Cut opening in fuselage part for horizontal stabilizer.

4 Score the fold lines for wing and tail tabs. (After cutting out the pieces, bend tabs outward.)

5 Cut each piece from the index card stock. Remove light-weight guide paper and discard, leaving a clean unmarked glider part.

NOTE: Cut carefully through both sheets. The cutting side is always the upward or outward facing surface of the finished part.

5L
4L
3L
2L
1F
2R
3R
4R
5R

6 Glue pieces 1F through 5R and 5L to build up fuselage layers, carefully aligning parts.

NOTE: Ensure that the entire contacting surface of a smaller piece being fastened to a larger one is completely covered with glue.

Press fuselage flat between clean sheets of paper underneath a heavy weight (a few big books) until glue is sufficiently set (about 45 minutes).

7 Bring wing parts 6R and 6L together, fastening with 7T. Then add 8R + 8L and 9R + 9L to the bottom of the wing. Finally glue 10B to the very bottom.

6L
7T
8L
9L
6R
8R
9R
10B

NOTE: Make sure wing parts are aligned along the centerline.

The dihedral angle of the wings must be set before the glue dries. See below.

8 Applying glue to the tail tabs, fasten horizontal stabilizer 11S to the fuselage.

11S

9 Applying glue to the wing tabs, fasten wing assembly to the fuselage.

10 Camber the wings by curving the paper gently between thumb and forefinger. See below.

point of maximum camber, 30% from front

Camber:

correct

too much

Dihedral: 1 3/4 in (4.5 cm)

NOTE: After completing the glider, it is important to let the glue set completely (an hour or two) before flying.

Waco CG-4

Parts

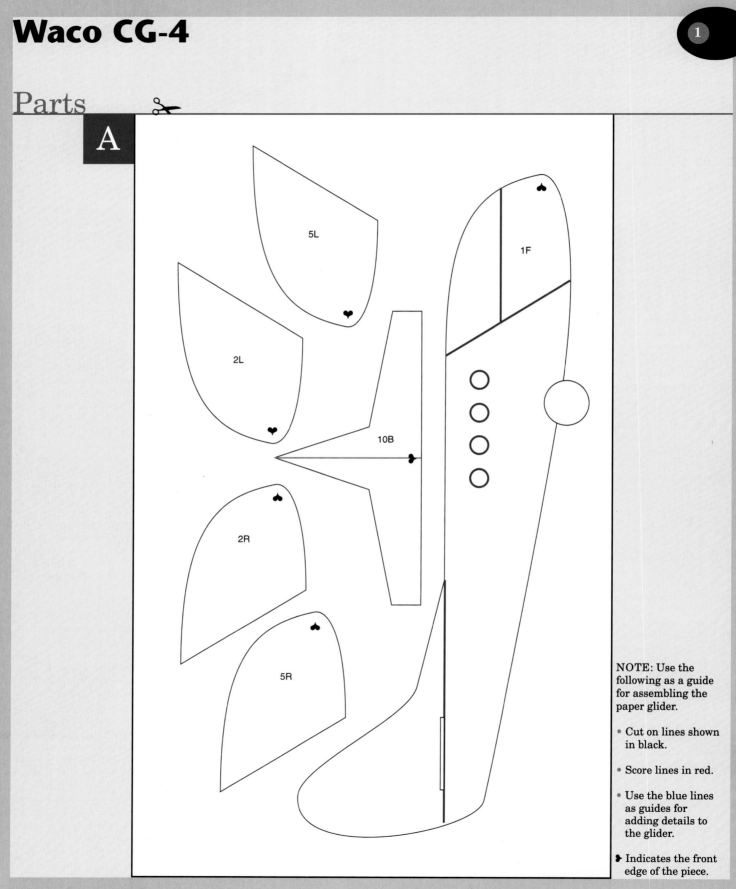

NOTE: Use the following as a guide for assembling the paper glider.

• Cut on lines shown in black.

• Score lines in red.

• Use the blue lines as guides for adding details to the glider.

❧ Indicates the front edge of the piece.

First, photocopy these two pages and the following two (100% size). Do not cut the pages from the book .

Then cut out the portion indicated below from the photocopy.
This makes a cutting guide for the various parts and fits a
standard 5 x 8 inch index card. See page 47 for step two.

Parts

B

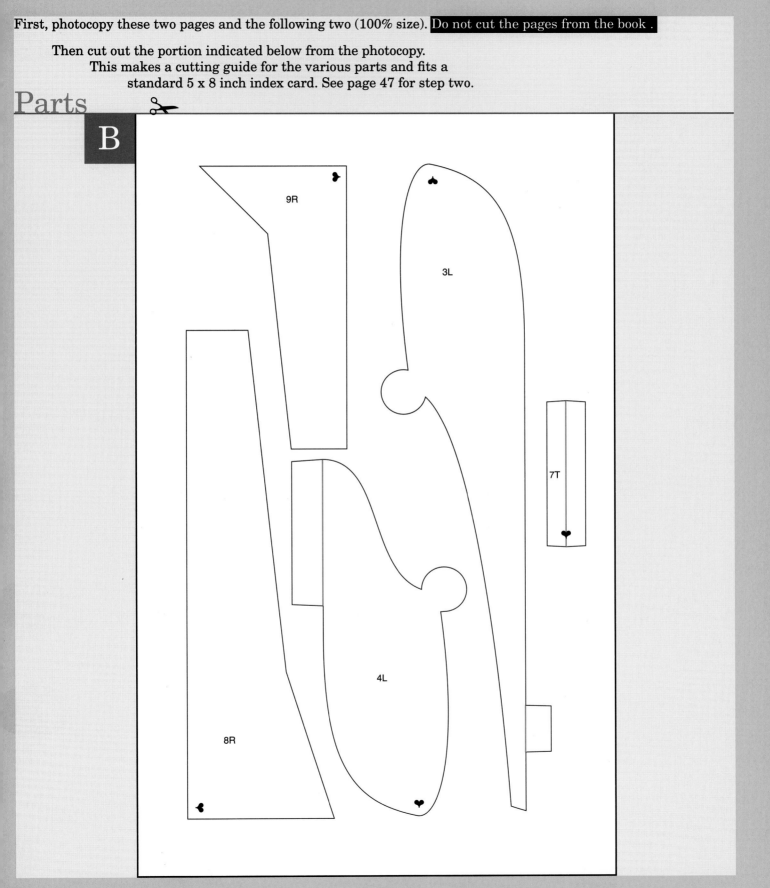

Parts

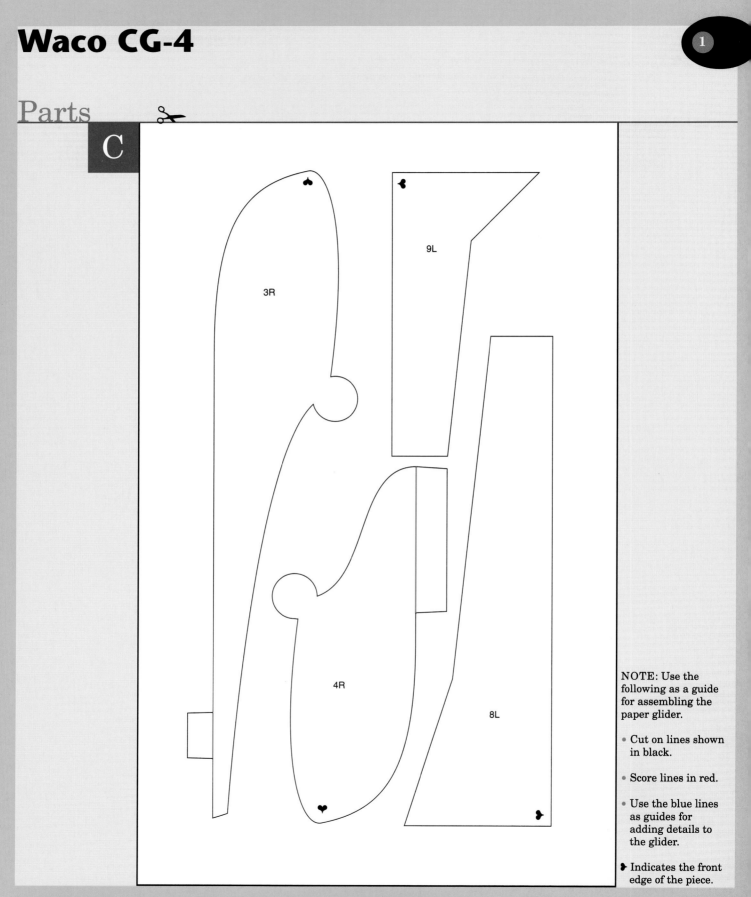

C

NOTE: Use the following as a guide for assembling the paper glider.

- Cut on lines shown in black.

- Score lines in red.

- Use the blue lines as guides for adding details to the glider.

- Indicates the front edge of the piece.

First, photocopy these two pages and the previous two (100% size). Do not cut the pages from the book .

Then cut out the portion indicated below from the photocopy.
This makes a cutting guide for the various parts and fits a
standard 5 x 8 inch index card. See page 47 for step two.

Parts

D

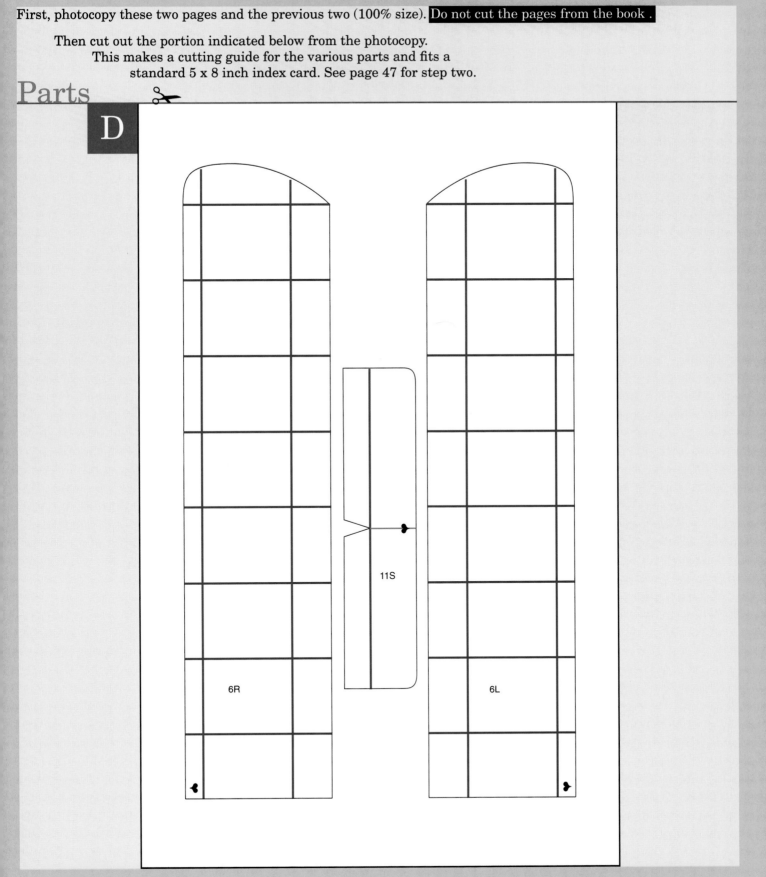

11S

6R

6L

Colditz Cock

8

This glider was designed and built by Allied prisoners in a German Prisoner of War Camp during the second world war as a means of escape. It could carry two people. Although the war ended before it was used, and the original glider disappeared after the war, a model has since been built and flown. **(See text p 56.)**

Instructions

NOTE: Also refer to general instructions on pp 6-9.

1 See pages 54 and 55 for this step.

2 Tack-glue parts cutting guides onto index cards by gluing on the **back-side between the parts**.

4 Cut each piece from the index card stock. Remove light-weight guide paper and discard, leaving a clean unmarked glider part.

NOTE: Cut carefully through both sheets. The cutting side is always the upward or outward facing surface of the finished part.

3 Score the fold lines for wing and tail tabs. (After cutting out the pieces, bend tabs outward.)

5 Glue pieces 1F through 8R and 8L to build up fuselage layers, carefully aligning parts.

NOTE: Ensure that the entire contacting surface of a smaller piece being fastened to a larger one is completely covered with glue.

Press fuselage flat between clean sheets of paper underneath a heavy weight (a few big books) until glue is sufficiently set (about 45 minutes).

6 Glue 10B to the bottom of wing part 9W.

9W

10B

7 Applying glue to the tail tabs, fasten horizontal stabilizer 11S to the fuselage.

11S

9 Camber the wings by curving the paper gently between thumb and forefinger. See below.

NOTE: Make sure wing parts are aligned along the centerline.

The dihedral angle of the wings must be set before the glue dries. See below.

8 Applying glue to the wing tabs, fasten wing assembly to the fuselage.

point of maximum camber, 30% from front

Camber:

correct

too much

Dihedral: ³/₄ in (2 cm)

NOTE: After completing the glider, it is important to let the glue set completely (an hour or two) before flying.

Colditz Cock

Parts

A

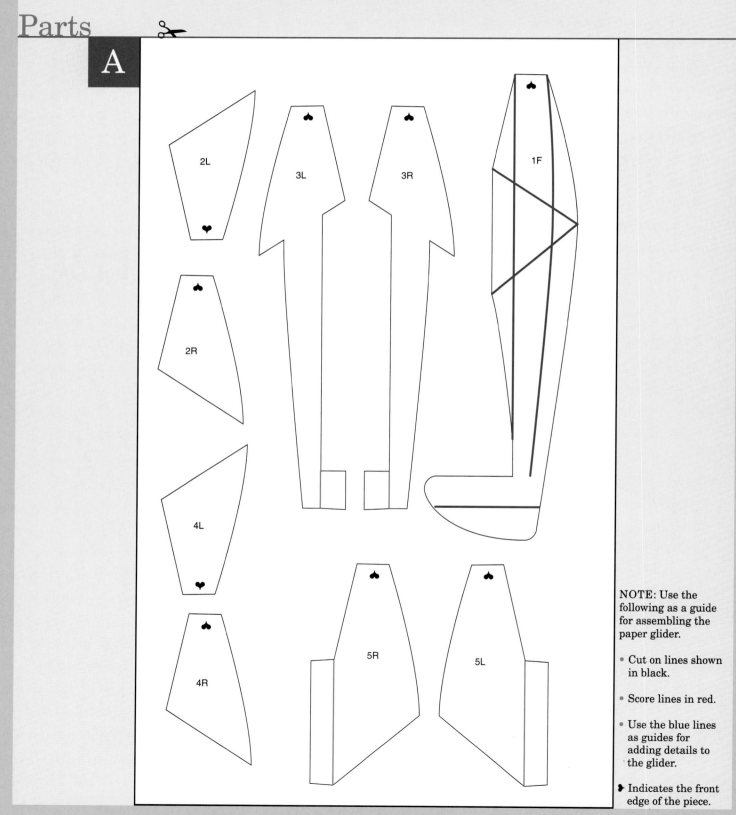

NOTE: Use the following as a guide for assembling the paper glider.

- Cut on lines shown in black.

- Score lines in red.

- Use the blue lines as guides for adding details to the glider.

❧ Indicates the front edge of the piece.

First, photocopy these two pages (100% size). Do not cut the pages from the book .

Then cut out the portion indicated below from the photocopy.
This makes a cutting guide for the various parts and fits a
standard 5 x 8 inch index card. See page 53 for step two.

Parts

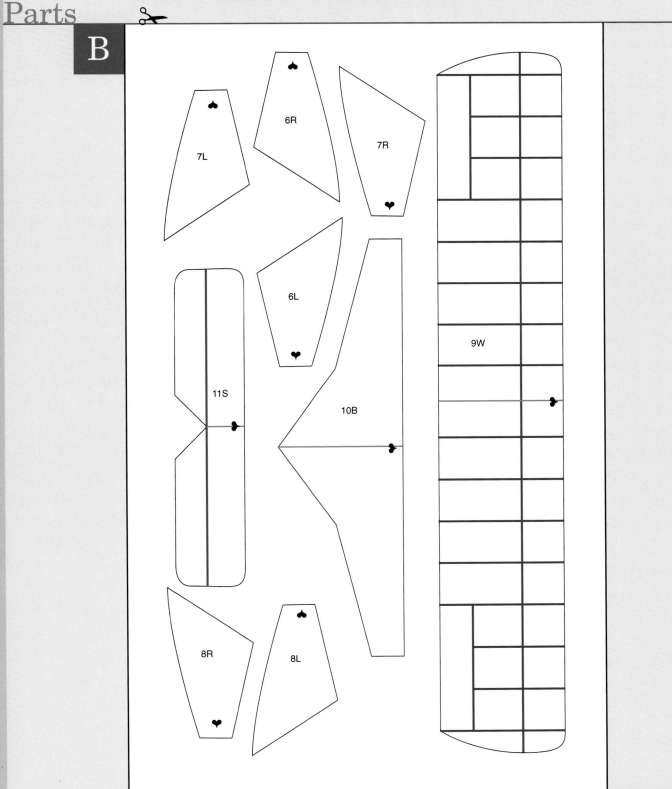

DURING the second world war Germany was first to make use of gliders for pilot training and the transport of troops and equipment. The Grunau Baby of the 1930s was a single seat glider in widespread use. More than 6000 of them were built. Many of the German Luftwaffe pilots had flown this glider prior to becoming fighter pilots. This was an important aircraft. Its popularity was instrumental in generating interest in gliding, not only in Germany, but across Europe. **(Paper glider 6, p 42.)**

In 1941 the U.S. government followed Germany's lead and undertook a nationwide glider training program. The Schweizer Aircraft Corporation was established at Elmira, New York to build gliders, and the first two-place instructional glider they made was selected as a military trainer, the TG-2.

Both sides in the conflict built combat gliders. The Allies had the British Horsa and the American Waco CG-4 for troop and equipment transport. Both were built in large numbers (14,000 CG-4s were built) and used for tactical battle maneuvers. The Axis had similar machines. All gliders were towed either singley or in pairs behind powered transport planes carrying paratroopers, and were used mainly for night invasion. Each of the gliders could carry about 5000 pounds (2250 kg) of equipment or troops. Once released from the tow plane, they could silently penetrate behind enemy lines.

The Horsa and the CG-4 played an important role in the liberation of Europe, with more than 500 gliders being flown in the initial invasion of Normandy in 1944. They were also used in other theaters of war, most notably in Burma, where 54 CG-4s took a force of engineers 100 miles behind enemy lines to establish a landing stronghold deep in the jungle. After one week they had successfully brought in 9,000 fully equipped troops. **(Paper glider 7, p 46.)**

During the war Colditz Castle, situated on the cliffs of Saxony, became a Prisoner of War camp. Bill Goldfinch, a British Flying Officer POW, designed a small glider which was built by fellow prisoners from materials in the camp and was to be used to escape the castle. Floorboards became wing spars, the ribs and frame were made from bed slats, and control lines were electrical wiring, all surreptitiously obtained. The covering was cotton which came from sleeping bags, sealed with a slurry made by boiling down prison ration millet. The war ended before the glider could be used but later a model was built and flown. **(Paper glider 8, p 52.)**

Figure 12
Soaring flight in wave lift

When air is forced upward over high mountains it behaves much like water that flows around stones in a river. Both form ripples and waves. These waves in air over mountains are often accompanied by lozenge-shaped clouds. A glider flown into wave lift can climb to extremely high altitudes — the very limits at which a human can live without a pressure suit. A supply of oxygen must be carried on board.

AFTER the war ended in 1945 aviators once again could turn to sport flying, and by the mid 1950s gliding and soaring had spread to most developed countries. The sport became well organized and the period was marked by research in material use, aerodynamics, meteorology, and soaring techniques.

As early as the mid-1930s German pilots had been aware of lift to very high altitudes near lozenge-shaped clouds over mountains. These clouds form as air is forced upward over mountain peaks and forms waves, much as ripples are formed around stones in a river. This source of lift is called *wave lift*. Before the days of aerotow launching it was difficult to reach. In 1947 Paul MacCready, flying an Orlik, climbed to an altitude of 21,000 feet (6300 m) over the Sierra Nevada mountains, beginning a trend at setting high altitude records. See figure 12.

The International Scientific and Technical Organization (OSTIV) made a standard body of research widely available, resulting in an increasing number of factory-built gliders for training and soaring.

Before the war German glider designers had experimented with lightweight alloy metal structures, slender fuselages with narrow eliptical cross-sections, small canopies, cantilevered (no bracing) high aspect ratio wings, and larger rudders. (For example, the Cirrus D-30, with a wingspan of 65 feet (20 m) and an aspect ratio of 33, whose performance was not surpassed until 1954.)

New world-wide research into materials and methods resulted in a widespread change in how gliders were built after the war. Great improvement could be achieved by using different airfoil cross-sectional shapes (see figure 13), and by reducing waviness in wings, using unbroken polished surfaces, adding rounded fairings, and removing even small gaps and air leaks.

The aspect ratio of wings and wing strength was constantly researched (see figure 14). World-wide research and sharing of knowledge led to the universal classification of sailplanes by performance levels. Standard Class defined the average sailplane. Mass produced sailplanes continually improved in quality and performance. Manufacturers used a variety of materials in sailplanes, often in one machine —wood, steel, aluminum, fabric, and fiberglass.

Immediately after the war most American glider manufacturers went out of business. Only the Schweizer Aircraft Corporation remained. Besides two-place training gliders, Schweizer also introduced high-performance single-seat sailplanes. Most glider pilots in North America since the mid 1950s have received their pilot training in a Schweizer glider.

War planes had been made mainly of metal — steel and alloy frames with lightweight riveted aluminum skins, yeilding good performance. This is the technology utilized by the Schweizers in glider construction. It proved to be ideal — the right weight for sailplanes, its strength afforded good pilot protection in the event of a crash, its smoothness gave the desired finish for reducing drag, and it was dura-

Figure 13
Airfoil cross-sections

Lilienthal used only a single skin over a curved frame, like an umbrella, to make wings for his gliders. Since the first world war there has been a steady evolution in the the cross-section shape of glider wings in the interest of creating higher lift to drag ratios and good performance. The thicker the wing, the greater the pressure drag. Also, the more difficult it is for air to flow smoothly around the curve. Different shapes operate at their own best angle of attack and airspeed. Therefore different thicknesses, positions of the point of maximum camber, shape of the lower surface, and positions of the trailing edge have been tried. Since the second world war wings have been made over which airflow closely follows the contour of the upper surface (laminar flow) for improved performance over a wider speed range. Some wings (not shown) have camber changing flaps at the trailing edge to decrease lift at higher speeds and increase it at lower speeds, giving the glider an even wider optimum speed range.

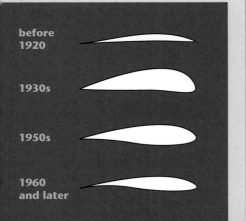

before 1920

1930s

1950s

1960 and later

Figure 14
The aspect ratio of sailplane wings

Research has proven that the longer a wing is in relation to the distance from its leading to trailing edge (higher aspect ratio) the greater its efficiency, having lower induced drag. Since the days of Lilienthal there has, therefore, been a steady increase in the aspect ratio of glider wings in the interest of improving glide ratios. The highest today is over 30:1. Most, however, are around 20. Correspondingly, wingspans, too, have increased. Most are between 48 and 54 feet (15-17 m). Greater spans make handling on the ground and in the air more difficult.

There is also a relationship between aspect ratio and a wing's thickness, as there is only so much strength that can be built into a wing of a given thickness. Early gliders all had struts to support the wings. Since the second world war, with the use of stronger materials, wings have been internally supported (cantilevered). In wings of high aspect ratio torsional strength, to keep them from distorting under load, requires careful and critical engineering.

High aspect ratio wings is one feature that distinguishes gliders from other aircraft.

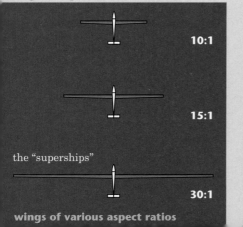

the "superships"

wings of various aspect ratios

10:1

15:1

30:1

ble. The Schweizers produced just the kind of gliders that would be attractive to the growing club market.

One Schweizer single-seat glider was the SGS 1-26. It had a steel tube frame with an alloy wing structure, aluminum and fabric skin, and a fiberglass nose. To keep costs down, it was originally planned as a kit, simple enough for the average person to assemble in the home garage without special tools. But soon it was produced also as a factory-built model. In total 700 of them were produced between 1954 and 1979.

It has become one of the most popular sailplanes in North America. Like the Grunau Baby in Europe, it was instrumental in popularizing the sport of soaring. Although it has been superseded in performance, and no longer ranks among the high-performance ships, most of the 1-26s built remain in active service as a favorite personal sport glider for many pilots, having become an "American Classic." It holds many records. The 1-26 Association was formed for pilots of this glider to exchange soaring ideas and to compete with one another. **(Paper glider 9, p 60.)**

Because aircraft designers were familiar with wood and fabric, and these materials were economical, gliders continued to be built from them. Skilled craftsmen were able to attain high performance using these materials. One example is the Sagitta, the first Standard Class sailplane produced in Holland. Another is the Schleicher Ka-6. It has become world famous for its good performance, winning the 1958 OSTIV award for the best Standard Class sailplane, as well as setting many flight records. **(Paper glider 10, p 64.)**

Some fine all-metal two-place gliders were built in Eastern Europe. One is the Blanik L-13, produced by the Czech Aeronautical Research Center. It is of steel and aluminum contruction with fabric covered control surfaces. Beginning in 1956 more than 2000 were produced. Outside of North America it remains the most common trainer and can be used for aerobatics. Another is the Lark from Romania. Because of its high performance, it has become popular world wide. It is also available as a single-seat model. **(Paper glider 11, p 68.)**

Among the innovations of the postwar period were flying wing sailplanes. In 1937 German engineer, Dr. Reimar Horton, built the first flying wing aircraft — aircraft without fuselages and whose wings provide both lift and stability. With some modifications, this configuration was utilized after the war by Witold Kasper, Jim Marske, and others. The Marske Pioneer, developed from a wood and fabric covered design of 1957, is popular in North America.

Mixed material construction yielded good sailplanes in all classes, but in 1964 the molded all-fiberglass Libelle was introduced by the German Glasflügel company, setting a new standard in smoothness.

Sailplanes and soaring at the end of the 20th century

BY the 1970s soaring had come of age, no longer limited to a few participants. The sport had grown sufficiently around the world that there were enough pilots of exceptional skill to warrant regular international competition, and many countries sent teams of their best to compete in the World Soaring Championships. In 1970 they were held in the United States for the first time and astronaut Niel Armstrong, who the year before had been first to land on the moon, was the official presidential representative at the event. He was the pilot of a Libelle 201 and a Schweizer 1-26.

It became apparent that the added performance of fiberglass ships was advantageous to pilots competing at national and international levels, and the composite construction techniques introduced by Glasflügel were copied by other manufacturers. The Standard Class became primarily a class of "glass slippers" — sleek fiberglass ships. Those manufacturers who did not adopt fiberglass went out of business or turned to other things — Schweizer no longer produces gliders.

In composite construction the frame is eliminated. Thin layers of strong fibers are molded into the glider's shape, infused with resin, and cured. This skin is strong, seamless, and smooth. With this technique Standard Class glide ratios increased from about 30:1 to nearly 40:1.

People have always enjoyed aerial displays. This prompted Ursula Hänle, whose husband designed the Libelle, to build a glider for just this purpose in 1971, the all-fiberglass Salto H-101. **(Paper glider 12, p 72.)**

Gliders with motors, for use when no source of lift can be found, were introduced. One example is the 1982 canard wing Solitaire, by Burt Rutan. The motor and propeller pop up out of its long nose when needed. **(Paper glider 13, p 76.)**

Composite construction is also compatible with computer aided design techniques, which allow for very precise aerodynamic measurements to be made. Jim Marske used this method for developing a new ultra-efficient glider, the Genesis, which was first flown in 1993. It is a hybrid design combining concepts from flying wing and regular aircraft. **(Paper glider 14, p 80.)**

By the mid 1980s the cost of Standard Class sailplanes had risen beyond the average person's reach, causing for the call of a new economical design. It was to be not only affordable but also a contender for Olympic competition. (Soaring is scheduled as an Olympic event in the year 2000.) A design competition was held. The winning design was the Polish PW-5 Smyk, certified in 1994. **(Paper glider 15, p 84.)**

Because soaring is a competitive sport, performance improvements at any cost continue to be made. Composite technology allows for the use of exotic materials such as kevlar and carbon fibers, having extraordinary strength for their weight, and allowing for the construction of ultra-high aspect ratio "superships" — gliders of exceptional performance. Examples are the Schleicher AS-W 22 and Schemp-Hirth Nimbus 4, the world's two highest performers, having glide ratios of over 60:1. **(Paper glider 16, p 88.)**

Schweizer SGS 1-26

9

The Schweizer SGS 1-26, first introduced as an economical glider to promote one-class competition in the early fifties, has become a favorite personal sport glider used for weekend recreational soaring as well as to set many records. Early models were metal framed with fabric covering, later ones were all metal. **(See text p 58.)**

Instructions

NOTE: Also refer to general instructions on pp 6-9.

1 See pages 62 and 63 for this step.

2 Tack-glue parts cutting guides onto index cards by gluing on the **back-side between the parts**.

3 Cut opening for wings in fuselage part.

4 Score the fold lines for wing and tail tabs. (After cutting out the pieces, bend tabs outward.)

5 Cut each piece from the index card stock. Remove light-weight guide paper and discard, leaving a clean unmarked glider part.

NOTE: Cut carefully through both sheets. The cutting side is always the upward or outward facing surface of the finished part.

6 Glue pieces 1F through 7R and 7L to build up fuselage layers, carefully aligning parts.

7L
6L
5L
4L
3L
2L
1F
2R
3R
4R
5R
6R
7R

NOTE: Ensure that the entire contacting surface of a smaller piece being fastened to a larger one is completely covered with glue.

Press fuselage flat between clean sheets of paper underneath a heavy weight (a few big books) until glue is sufficiently set (about 45 minutes).

7 Bring wing parts 8R and 8L together, fastening with 9T. Then glue 10M to the bottom of the wing. Finally glue 11B to the very bottom.

9T
8L
10M
8R
11B

8 Applying glue to the tail tabs, fasten horizontal stabilizer 12S to the fuselage.

12S

10 Camber the wings by curving the paper gently between thumb and forefinger. See below.

NOTE: Make sure wing parts are aligned along the centerline.

The dihedral angle of the wings must be set before the glue dries. See below.

9 Applying glue to the wing tabs, fasten wing assembly to the fuselage.

Camber:

point of maximum camber, 30% from front

correct

too much

Dihedral: 1 in (2.5 cm)

NOTE: After completing the glider, it is important to let the glue set completely (an hour or two) before flying.

Schweizer SGS 1-26

Parts

A

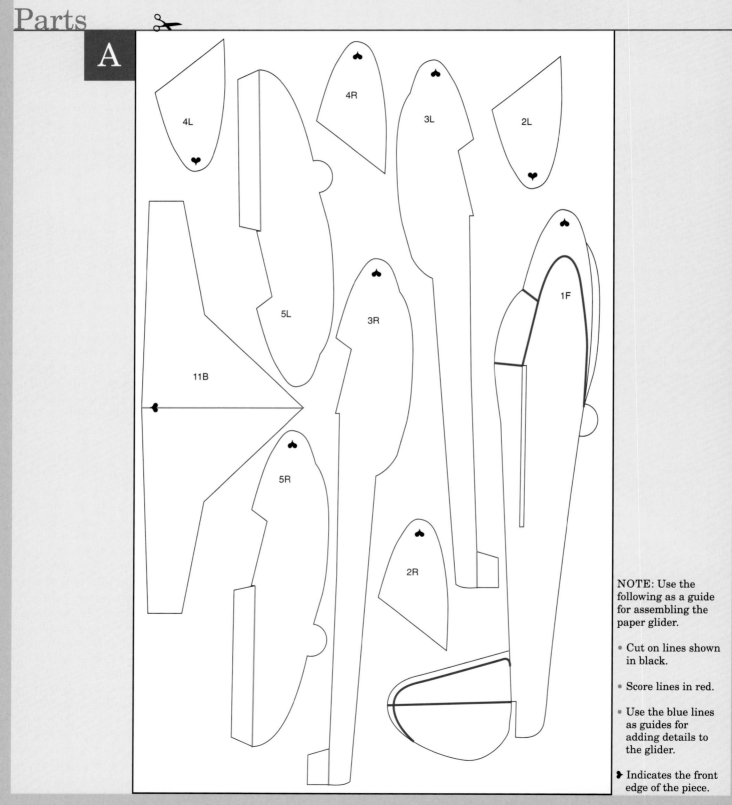

NOTE: Use the following as a guide for assembling the paper glider.

- Cut on lines shown in black.

- Score lines in red.

- Use the blue lines as guides for adding details to the glider.

♪ Indicates the front edge of the piece.

First, photocopy these two pages (100% size). Do not cut the pages from the book .

Then cut out the portion indicated below from the photocopy.
This makes a cutting guide for the various parts and fits a
standard 5 x 8 inch index card. See page 61 for step two.

Parts

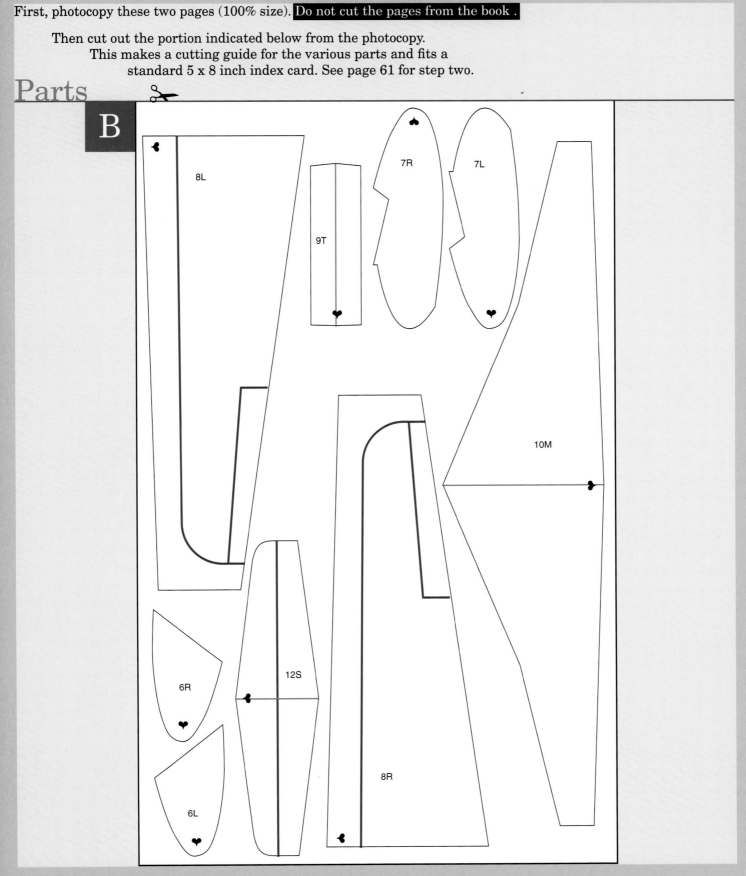

Schleicher Ka-6

10

This is an all-wood aircraft, including most of the covering. It has become world famous for its many accomplishments, winning awards for both design and good flights. In 1963 two were flown from Germany to France for a world distance record that stood until 1969. More than 500 were built. **(See text p 58.)**

Instructions

NOTE: Also refer to general instructions on pp 6-9.

1 See pages 66 and 67 for this step.

2 Tack-glue parts cutting guides onto index cards by gluing on the **back-side between the parts**.

3 Cut opening in fuselage part for horizontal stabilizer.

5 Cut each piece from the index card stock. Remove light-weight guide paper and discard, leaving a clean unmarked glider part.

4 Score the fold lines for wing and tail tabs. (After cutting out the pieces, bend tabs outward.)

NOTE: Cut carefully through both sheets. The cutting side is always the upward or outward facing surface of the finished part.

NOTE: Ensure that the entire contacting surface of a smaller piece being fastened to a larger one is completely covered with glue.

6 Glue pieces 1F through 4R and 4L to build up fuselage layers, carefully aligning parts.

4L
3L
2L
1F
2R
3R
4R

Press fuselage flat between clean sheets of paper underneath a heavy weight (a few big books) until glue is sufficiently set (about 45 minutes).

7 Bring wing parts 5R and 5L together, fastening with 6T. Then glue 7R and 7L to the bottom of the wing. Finally glue 8B to the very bottom.

6T
5L
7L
5R
7R
8B

8 Applying glue to the tail tabs, fasten horizontal stabilizer 9S to the fuselage.

10 Camber the wings by curving the paper gently between thumb and forefinger. See below.

9S

NOTE: Make sure wing parts are aligned along the centerline.

The dihedral angle of the wings must be set before the glue dries. See below.

9 Applying glue to the wing tabs, fasten wing assembly to the fuselage.

point of maximum camber, 30% from front

Camber:

correct

too much

Dihedral: 1 ¹/₂ in (3.75 cm)

NOTE: After completing the glider, it is important to let the glue set completely (an hour or two) before flying.

Schleicher Ka-6

Parts

A

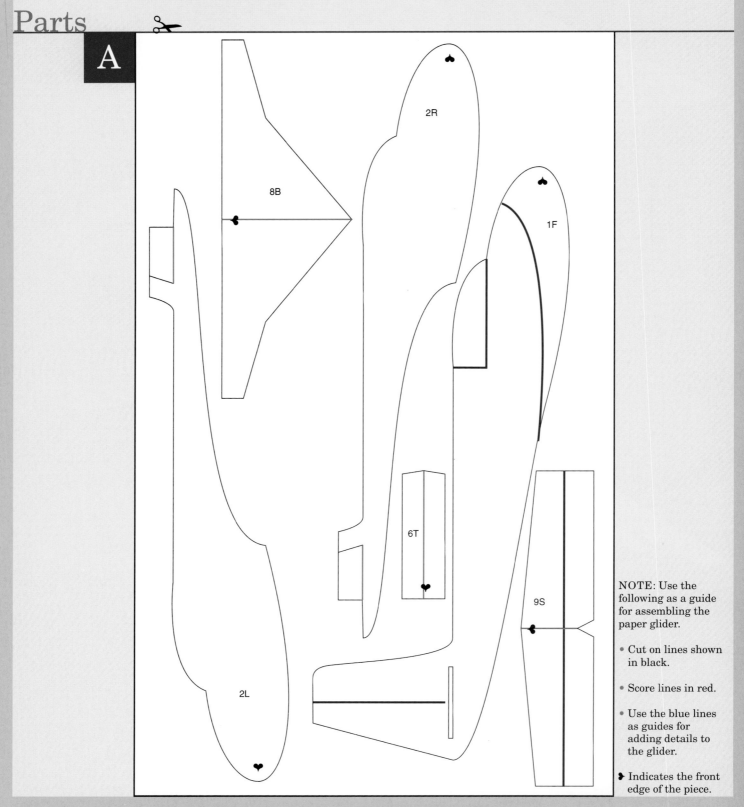

NOTE: Use the following as a guide for assembling the paper glider.

• Cut on lines shown in black.

• Score lines in red.

• Use the blue lines as guides for adding details to the glider.

❥ Indicates the front edge of the piece.

First, photocopy these two pages (100% size). Do not cut the pages from the book .

Then cut out the portion indicated below from the photocopy.
This makes a cutting guide for the various parts and fits a
standard 5 x 8 inch index card. See page 65 for step two.

Parts

B

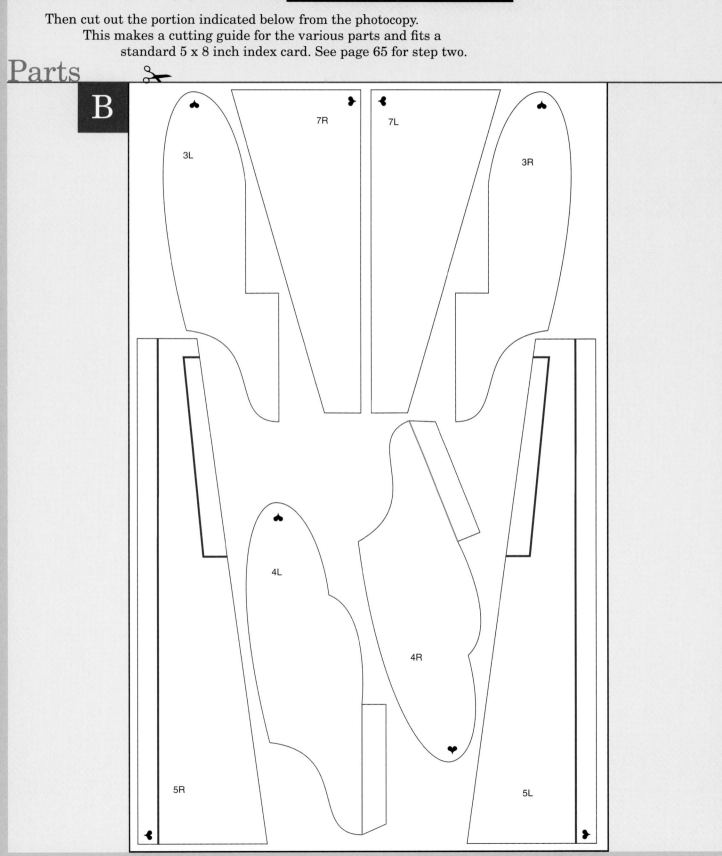

Lark I.S. 28B2

11

This large two-place glider is of all-metal construction and has a gross weight of 1300 pounds (585 kg). Despite its large size, it has good performance with camber changing flaps on its wings. More than 300 of this glider have been produced. It is also available in a smaller single-seat model, the I.S.29D2. **(See text p 58.)**

NOTE: Also refer to general instructions on pp 6-9.

1 See pages 70 and 71 for this step.

2 Tack-glue parts cutting guides onto index cards by gluing on the **back-side between the parts**.

4 Cut each piece from the index card stock. Remove light-weight guide paper and discard, leaving a clean unmarked glider part.

NOTE: Cut carefully through both sheets. The cutting side is always the upward or outward facing surface of the finished part.

3 Score the fold lines for wing and tail tabs. (After cutting out the pieces, bend tabs outward.)

5 Glue pieces 1F through 5R and 5L to build up fuselage layers, carefully aligning parts.

NOTE: Ensure that the entire contacting surface of a smaller piece being fastened to a larger one is completely covered with glue.

Press fuselage flat between clean sheets of paper underneath a heavy weight (a few big books) until glue is sufficiently set (about 45 minutes).

5L
4L
3L
2L
1F
2R
3R
4R
5R

6 Bring wing parts 6R and 6L together, fastening with 7T. Then add 8R + 8L and 9R + 9L to the bottom of the wing. Finally glue 10B to the very bottom.

7T
6L
8L
9L
6R
8R
9R
10B
11S

7 Applying glue to the tail tabs, fasten horizontal stabilizer 11S to the fuselage.

9 Camber the wings by curving the paper gently between thumb and forefinger. See below.

NOTE: Make sure wing parts are aligned along the centerline.

The dihedral angle of the wings must be set before the glue dries. See below.

8 Applying glue to the wing tabs, fasten wing assembly to the fuselage.

point of maximum camber, 30% from front

Camber:

correct

too much

Dihedral: 1 $\frac{1}{2}$ in (3.75 cm)

NOTE: After completing the glider, it is important to let the glue set completely (an hour or two) before flying.

Parts

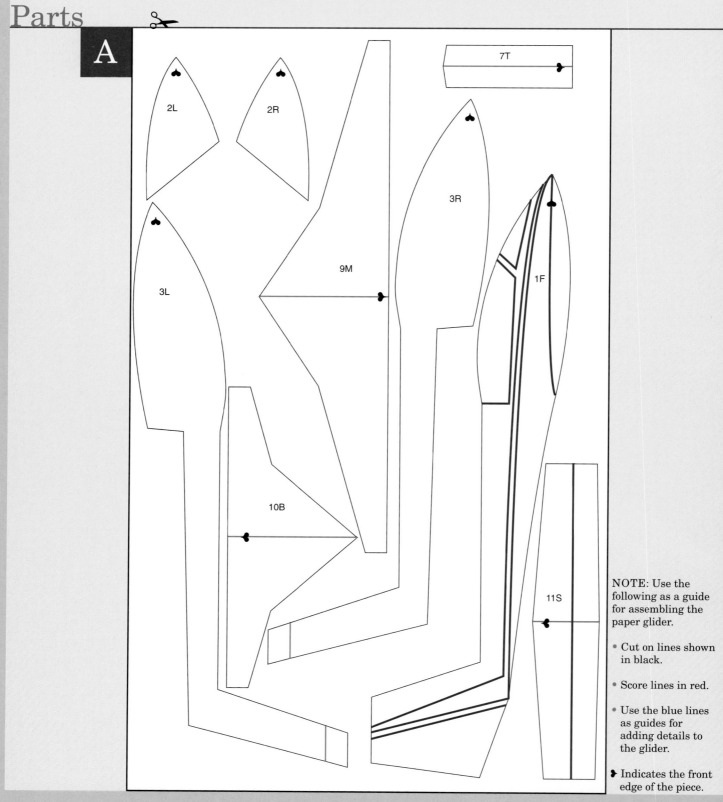

A

7T

2L

2R

3R

3L

9M

1F

10B

11S

NOTE: Use the following as a guide for assembling the paper glider.

• Cut on lines shown in black.

• Score lines in red.

• Use the blue lines as guides for adding details to the glider.

➤ Indicates the front edge of the piece.

First, photocopy these two pages (100% size). 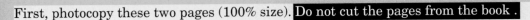Do not cut the pages from the book .

Then cut out the portion indicated below from the photocopy.
This makes a cutting guide for the various parts and fits a
standard 5 x 8 inch index card. See page 69 for step two.

Parts

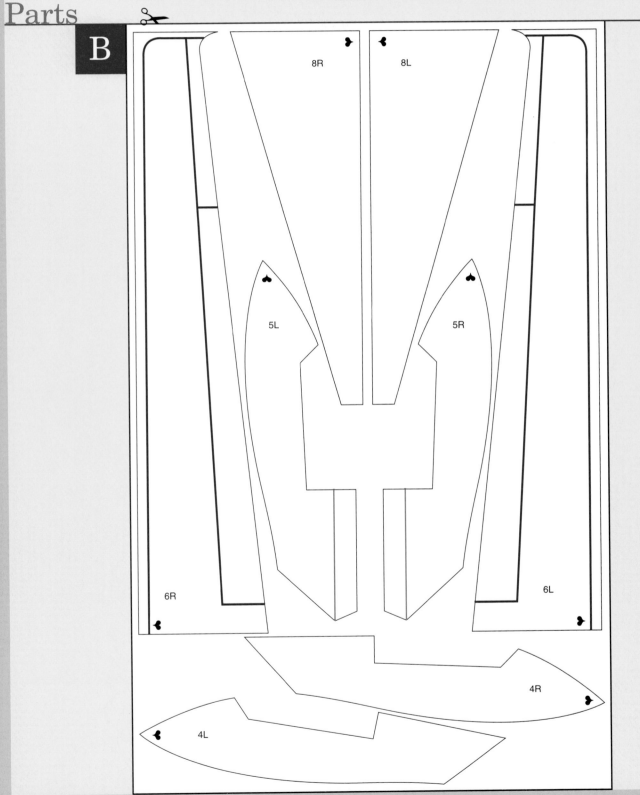

B

8R   8L

5L   5R

6R   6L

4R

4L

Salto H-101

12

Salto means summersault in German. This all-fiberglass glider is designed to do aerobatic flying. Since the early days of aviation people have been thrilled by the sight of aerial displays consisting of rolls, loops, and spins. For maneuverability this glider has a relatively short wingspan and a large V-shaped tail. It uses some parts in common with the Libelle. **(See text p 59.)**

Instructions

NOTE: Also refer to general instructions on pp 6-9.

1 — See pages 74 and 75 for this step.

2 — Tack-glue parts cutting guides onto index cards by gluing on the **back-side between the parts**.

3 — Cut opening for wings in fuselage part.

5 — Cut each piece from the index card stock. Remove light-weight paper and discard, leaving a clean unmarked glider part.

NOTE: Cut carefully through both sheets. The cutting side is always the upward or outward facing surface of the finished part.

4 — Score the fold lines for wing and tail tabs. (After cutting out the pieces, bend tabs outward.)

NOTE: Ensure that the entire contacting surface of a smaller piece being fastened to a larger one is completely covered with glue.

6 — Glue pieces 1F through 6R and 6L to build up fuselage layers, carefully aligning parts.

Press fuselage flat between clean sheets of paper underneath a heavy weight (a few big books) until glue is sufficiently set (about 45 minutes).

7 — Bring wing parts 7R and 7L together, fastening with 8T. Then glue 9R and 9L to the bottom of the wing. Finally glue 10B to the very bottom.

8 — Applying glue to the tail tabs and fasten V-tail 11V to the fuselage, adjusting dihedral to 45 degrees.

10 — Camber the wings by curving the paper gently between thumb and forefinger. See below.

NOTE: Make sure wing parts are aligned along the centerline.

The dihedral angle of the wings must be set before the glue dries. See below.

9 — Applying glue to the wing tabs, fasten wing assembly to the fuselage.

Camber:

point of maximum camber, 30% from front

correct

too much

Dihedral: 1 $\frac{1}{4}$ in (3 cm)

NOTE: After completing the glider, it is important to let the glue set completely (an hour or two) before flying.

Salto H-101

Parts

A

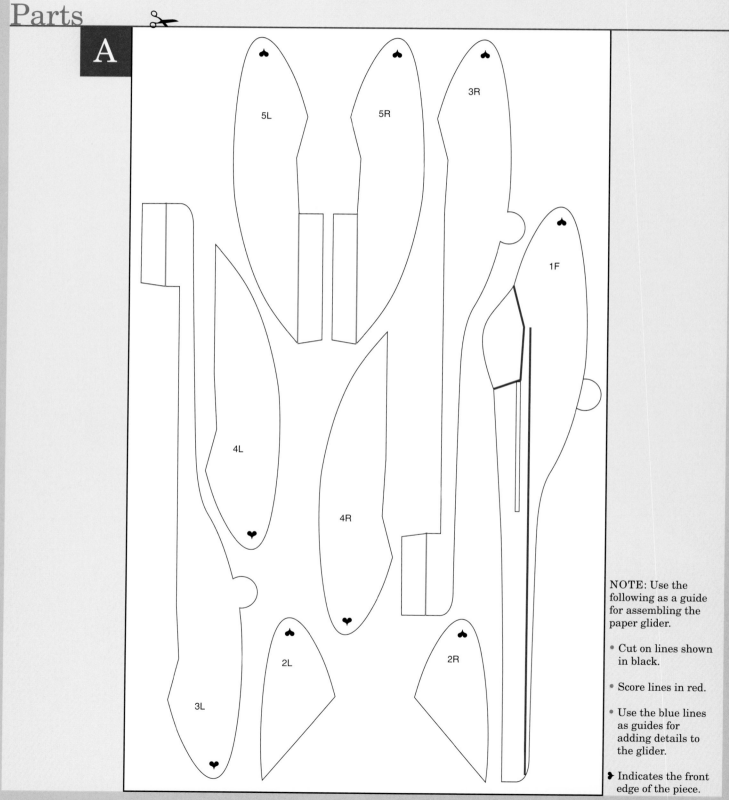

NOTE: Use the following as a guide for assembling the paper glider.

- Cut on lines shown in black.

- Score lines in red.

- Use the blue lines as guides for adding details to the glider.

➤ Indicates the front edge of the piece.

First, photocopy these two pages (100% size). Do not cut the pages from the book .

Then cut out the portion indicated below from the photocopy.
This makes a cutting guide for the various parts and fits a
standard 5 x 8 inch index card. See page 73 for step two.

Parts

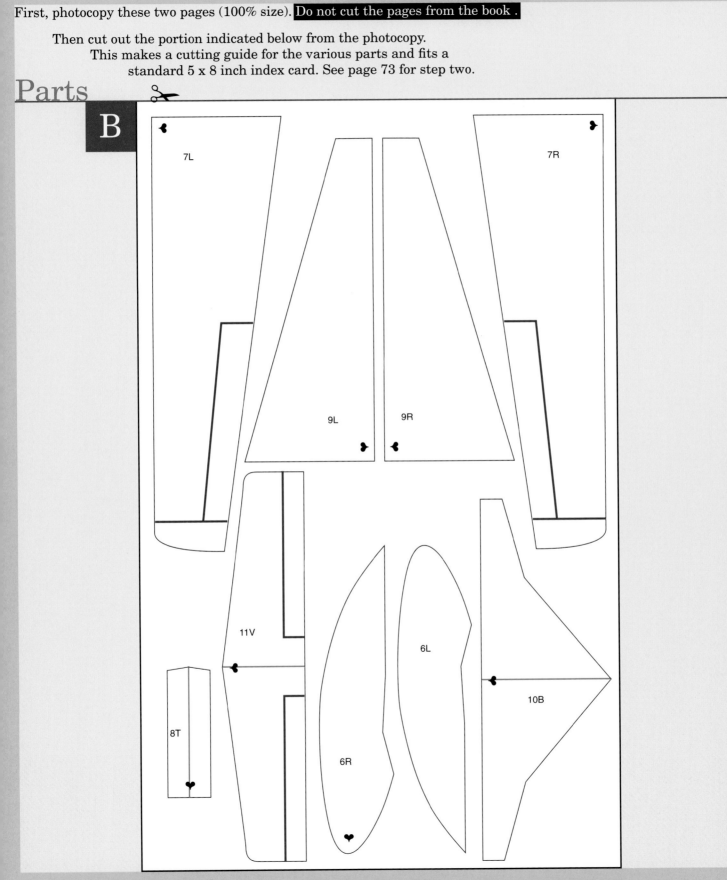

Solitaire Canard

Canards have small wings ahead of the main ones, necessitating a longer nose, which makes the planes look like long-necked ducks. (Canard means duck in French.) Aircraft designer, Burt Rutan, is known for his wide variety of canard aircraft. This glider is unusual not only because it is a canard, but also because it is a motorglider, which allows it to remain aloft even when no sources of lift are present. It is of all-fiberglass construction. **(See text p 59.)**

Instructions

NOTE: Also refer to general instructions on pp 6-9.

1 See pages 78 and 79 for this step.

2 Tack-glue parts cutting guides onto index cards by gluing on the **back-side between the parts**.

3 Cut opening for wings in fuselage parts.

5 Cut each piece from the index card stock. Remove light-weight guide paper and discard, leaving a clean unmarked glider part.

4 Score the fold lines for wing and tail tabs. (After cutting out the pieces, bend tabs outward.)

NOTE: Cut carefully through both sheets. The cutting side is always the upward or outward facing surface of the finished part.

6L
5L
4L
3L
2L
1F
2R
1F
3R
4R
5R
6R

7 Glue 12B to the bottom of the canard wing piece 11C.

11C
12B

NOTE: Ensure that the entire contacting surface of a smaller piece being fastened to a larger one is completely covered with glue.

6 Glue pieces 1F through 6R and 6L to build up fuselage layers, carefully aligning parts.

Press fuselage flat between clean sheets of paper underneath a heavy weight (a few big books) until glue is sufficiently set (about 45 minutes).

8 Bring wing parts 7R and 7L together, fastening with 8T. Then glue 9R and 9L to the bottom of the wing. Finally glue 10B to the very bottom.

7L
8T
9L
7R
9R
10B

9 Applying glue to the wing tabs, fasten main wing assembly to the fuselage.

11 Camber the wings by curving the paper gently between thumb and forefinger. See below.

NOTE: Make sure wing parts are aligned along the centerline.

The dihedral angle of the wings must be set before the glue dries. See below.

10 Applying glue to the wing tabs, fasten canard wing assembly to the fuselage.

Camber:

point of maximum camber, 30% from front

correct

too much

Dihedral: 1 $\frac{1}{4}$ in (3 cm)

NOTE: After completing the glider, it is important to let the glue set completely (an hour or two) before flying.

Solitaire Canard

Parts

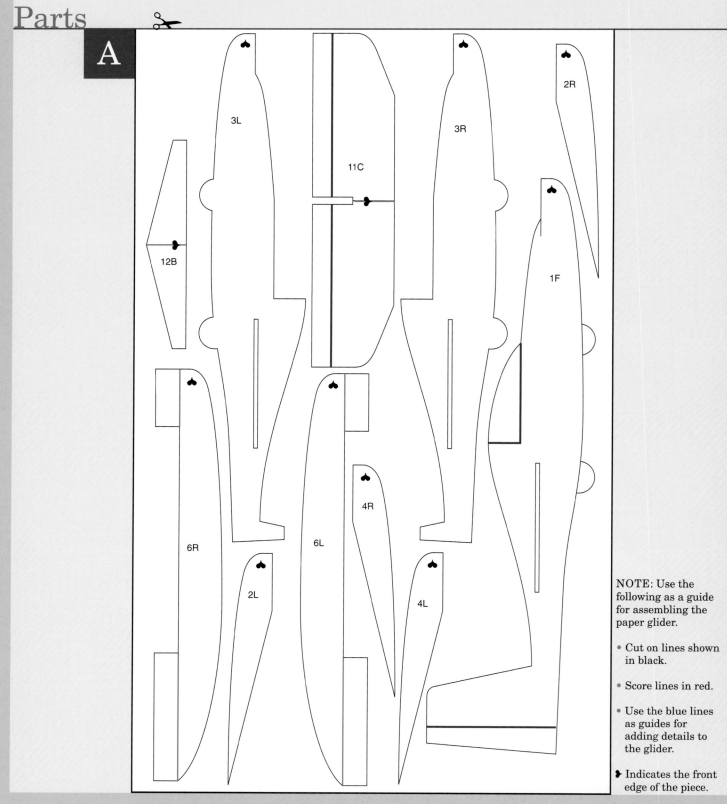

A

NOTE: Use the following as a guide for assembling the paper glider.

- Cut on lines shown in black.

- Score lines in red.

- Use the blue lines as guides for adding details to the glider.

❧ Indicates the front edge of the piece.

First, photocopy these two pages (100% size). Do not cut the pages from the book .

Then cut out the portion indicated below from the photocopy.
This makes a cutting guide for the various parts and fits a
standard 5 x 8 inch index card. See page 77 for step two.

Parts

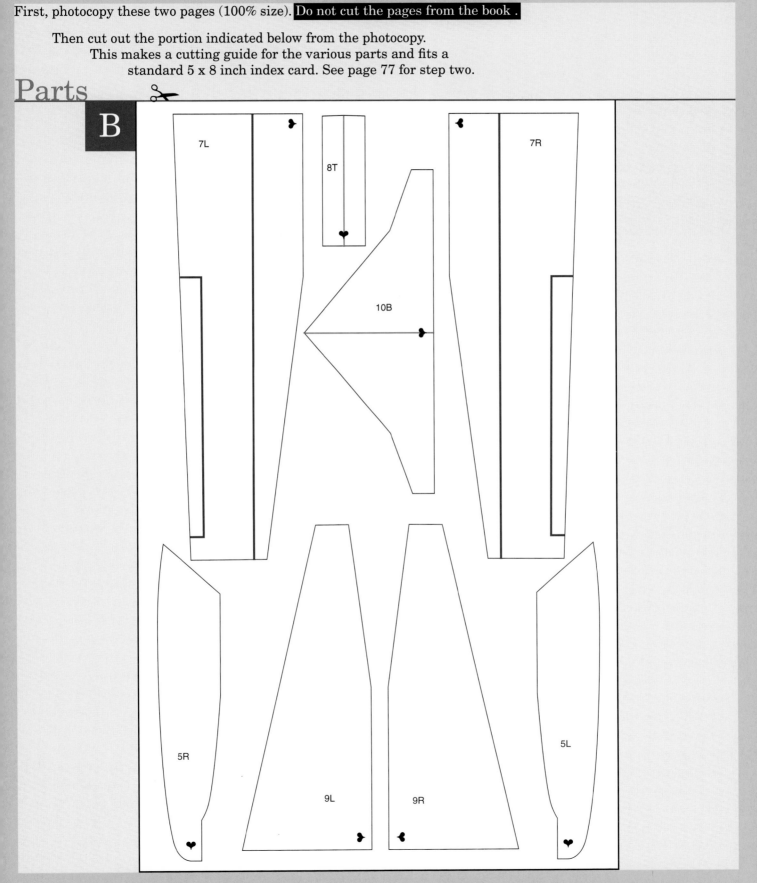

Genesis

Jim Marske has been building flying wing aircraft since the 1950s, experimenting with different designs. For the development of this glider he lent his expertise to a team of designers. The result was a hybrid with some features of a regular aircraft, such as vertical and horizontal stabilizers, but with virtually no fuselage like a flying wing. The team used the computer to develop its aerodynamics. Computer assisted design makes very efficient low drag airframes possible. This glider is of fiberglass and kevlar construction. **(See text p 59.)**

Instructions

NOTE: Also refer to general instructions on pp 6-9.

1 See pages 82 and 83 for this step.

2 Tack-glue parts cutting guides onto index cards by gluing on the **back-side between the parts**.

3 Cut opening for wings in fuselage parts.

4 Score the fold lines for wing and tail tabs. (After cutting out the pieces, bend tabs outward.)

5 Cut each piece from the index card stock. Remove light-weight guide paper and discard, leaving a clean unmarked glider part.

NOTE: Cut carefully through both sheets. The cutting side is always the upward or outward facing surface of the finished part.

NOTE: Ensure that the entire contacting surface of a smaller piece being fastened to a larger one is completely covered with glue.

6 Glue pieces 1F through 5R and 5L to build up fuselage layers, carefully aligning parts.

Press fuselage flat between clean sheets of paper underneath a heavy weight (a few big books) until glue is sufficiently set (about 45 minutes).

7 Bring wing parts 6R and 6L together, fastening with 7T. Then glue 8R and 8L to the bottom of the wing. Finally glue 9B to the very bottom.

8 Applying glue to the tail tabs, fasten horizontal stabilizer 10S to the fuselage.

10 Camber the wings by curving the paper gently between thumb and forefinger. See below.

NOTE: Make sure wing parts are aligned along the centerline.

The dihedral angle of the wings must be set before the glue dries. See below.

9 Applying glue to the wing tabs, fasten wing assembly to the fuselage.

Camber:

point of maximum camber, 30% from front

correct

too much

Dihedral: 2 in (5 cm)

NOTE: After completing the glider, it is important to let the glue set completely (an hour or two) before flying.

5L
4L
3L
2L
1F
2R
3R
4R
5R

7T
6L
8L
6R
8R
9B
10S

Genesis

Parts ✂

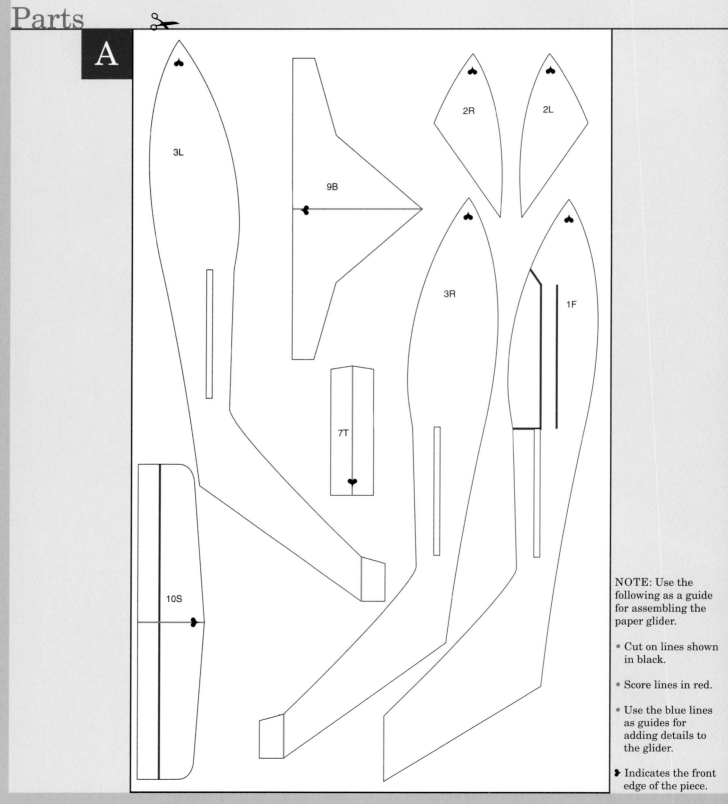

A

3L

2R   2L

9B

3R   1F

7T

10S

NOTE: Use the
following as a guide
for assembling the
paper glider.

• Cut on lines shown
  in black.

• Score lines in red.

• Use the blue lines
  as guides for
  adding details to
  the glider.

❦ Indicates the front
  edge of the piece.

First, photocopy these two pages (100% size). Do not cut the pages from the book .

Then cut out the portion indicated below from the photocopy.
This makes a cutting guide for the various parts and fits a
standard 5 x 8 inch index card. See page 81 for step two.

Parts

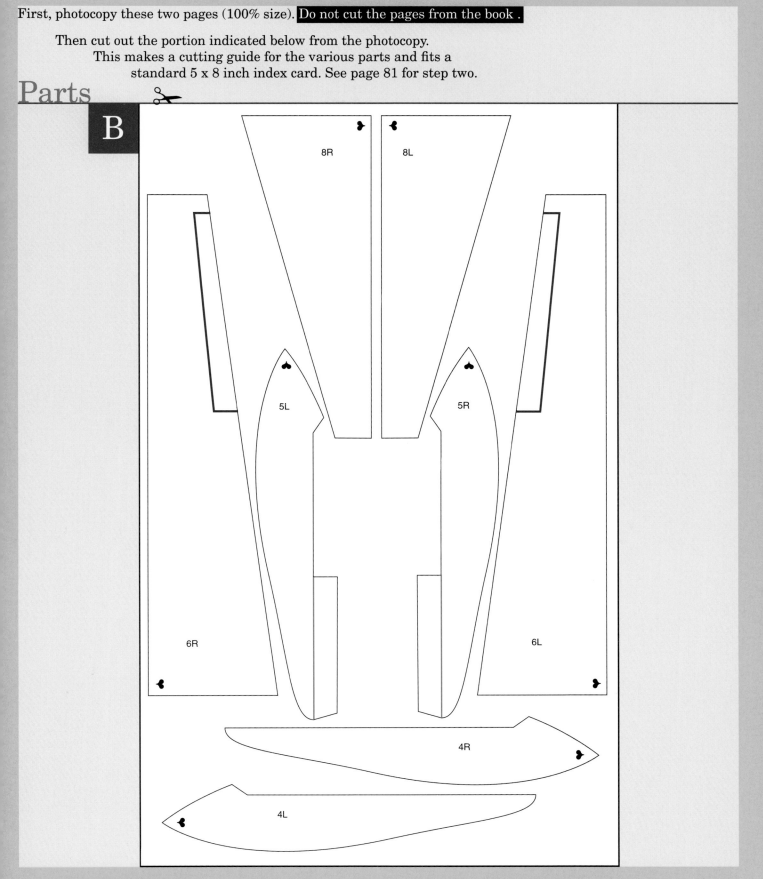

PW-5 Smyk

This glider, designed by the Warsaw Technical University in 1993 and certified the following year, introduces a new World Class sailplane. It is designed to be flown by all competing pilots in the Olympic Games of the year 2000, making one-class competition, begun in the U.S. by the Schweizer 1-26, into a world-wide concept. It is designed to be economical — half the cost of a Standard Class glider. It is of all-fiberglass construction, with flight characteristics suited for pilots of all skill levels. **(See text p 59.)**

Instructions

NOTE: Also refer to general instructions on pp 6-9.

1 See pages 86 and 87 for this step.

2 Tack-glue parts cutting guides onto index cards by gluing on the **back-side between the parts**.

3 Cut opening for wings in fuselage part.

4 Score the fold lines for wing and tail tabs. (After cutting out the pieces, bend tabs outward.)

5 Cut each piece from the index card stock. Remove light-weight guide paper and discard, leaving a clean unmarked glider part.

NOTE: Cut carefully through both sheets. The cutting side is always the upward or outward facing surface of the finished part.

6 Glue pieces 1F through 6R and 6L to build up fuselage layers, carefully aligning parts.

NOTE: Ensure that the entire contacting surface of a smaller piece being fastened to a larger one is completely covered with glue.

Press fuselage flat between clean sheets of paper underneath a heavy weight (a few big books) until glue is sufficiently set (about 45 minutes).

6L
5L
4L
3L
2L
1F
2R
3R
4R
5R
6R

7 Bring wing parts 7R and 7L together, fastening with 8T. Then glue 9R and 9L to the bottom of the wing. Finally glue 10B to the very bottom.

7L
8T
9L
7R
9R
10B

NOTE: Make sure wing parts are aligned along the centerline.

The dihedral angle of the wings must be set before the glue dries. See below.

8 Applying glue to the tail tabs, fasten horizontal stabilizer 11S to the fuselage.

11S

9 Applying glue to the wing tabs, fasten wing assembly to the fuselage.

10 Camber the wings by curving the paper gently between thumb and forefinger. See below.

point of maximum camber, 30% from front

Camber:

correct

too much

Dihedral: 1 ¹/₂ in (3.75 cm)

NOTE: After completing the glider, it is important to let the glue set completely (an hour or two) before flying.

PW-5 Smyk

Parts

A

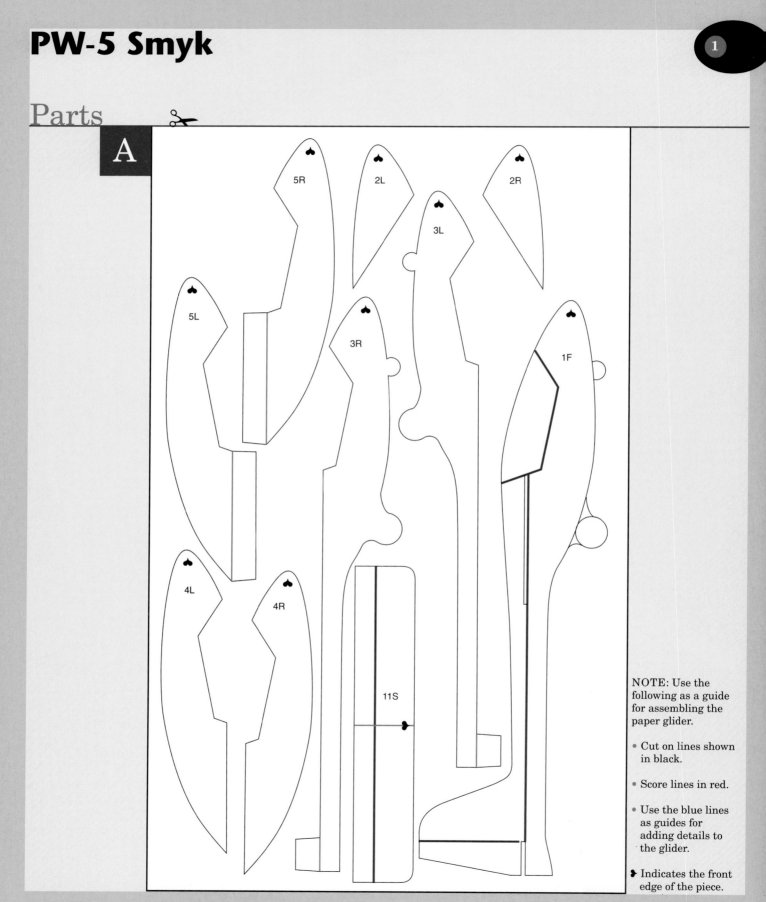

5R   2L   2R

3L

5L   3R   1F

4L   4R

11S

NOTE: Use the following as a guide for assembling the paper glider.

- Cut on lines shown in black.

- Score lines in red.

- Use the blue lines as guides for adding details to the glider.

➤ Indicates the front edge of the piece.

First, photocopy these two pages (100% size). Do not cut the pages from the book.

Then cut out the portion indicated below from the photocopy.
This makes a cutting guide for the various parts and fits a
standard 5 x 8 inch index card. See page 85 for step two.

Parts

B

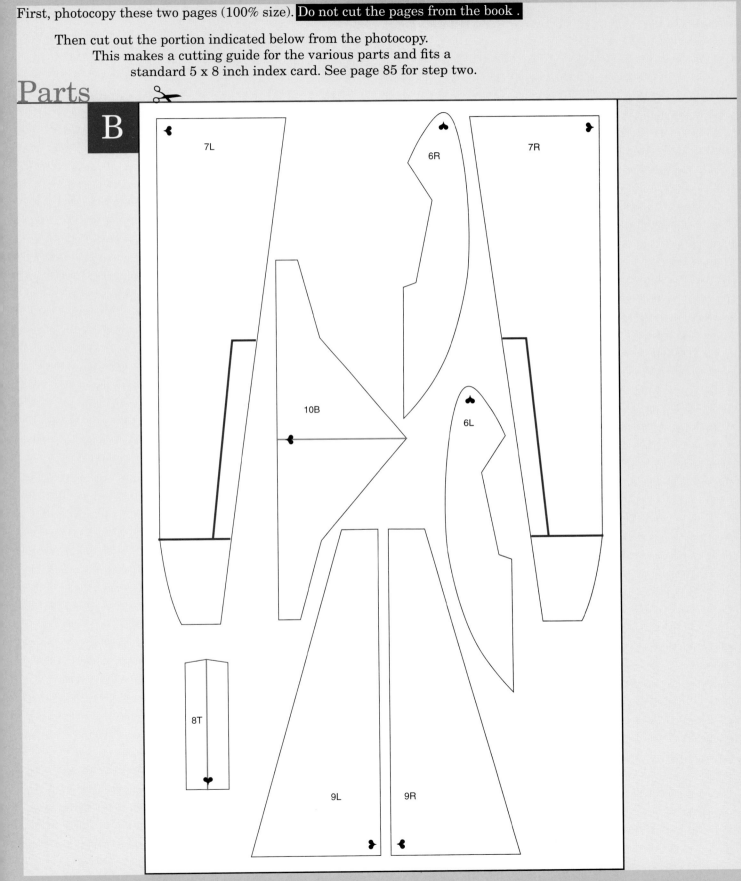

Schemp-Hirth Nimbus 4

16

This "supership" is a champion Open Class sailplane, sought after by world-class pilots. Shortly after its introduction, it ranked highest in the first 6 places and second in 9 out of the next 12 in the 1983 World Soaring Championships. This superb aircraft is of carbon fiber construction. It is also available with a motor that pops out of the fuselage behind the cockpit allowing it to remain airborne when no sources of lift are present. **(See text p 59.)**

Instructions

1 See pages 90 through 92 for this step.

2 Tack-glue parts cutting guides onto index cards by gluing on the **back-side between the parts**.

3 Cut opening for wings in fuselage parts.

5 Cut each piece from the index card stock. Remove light-weight guide paper and discard, leaving a clean unmarked glider part.

NOTE: Cut carefully through both sheets. The cutting side is always the upward or outward facing surface of the finished part.

4 Score the fold lines for wing and tail tabs. (After cutting out the pieces, bend tabs outward.)

6 Glue pieces 1F through 6R and 6L to build up fuselage layers, carefully aligning parts.

NOTE: Ensure that the entire contacting surface of a smaller piece being fastened to a larger one is completely covered with glue.

Press fuselage flat between clean sheets of paper underneath a heavy weight (a few big books) until glue is sufficiently set (about 45 minutes).

7 Bring wing parts 7R and 7L together, fastening with 8T. Then add 9R + 9L and 10R + 10L to the bottom of the wing. Finally glue 11B and 12B to the very bottom.

8 Applying glue to the tail tabs, fasten horizontal stabilizer 13S to the fuselage.

10 Camber the wings by curving the paper gently between thumb and forefinger. See below.

NOTE: Make sure wing parts are aligned along the centerline.

The dihedral angle of the wings must be set before the glue dries. See below.

9 Applying glue to the wing tabs, fasten wing assembly to the fuselage.

point of maximum camber, 30% from front

Camber:

correct

too much

NOTE: After completing the glider, it is important to let the glue set completely (an hour or two) before flying.

Dihedral: 2 ³/₄ in (7 cm)

6L
5L
4L
3L
2L
1F
2R
3R
4R
5R
6R

7L
8T
9L
10L
11L
9R
10R
11R
12B
13S
7R

Schemp-Hirth Nimbus 4

Parts

A

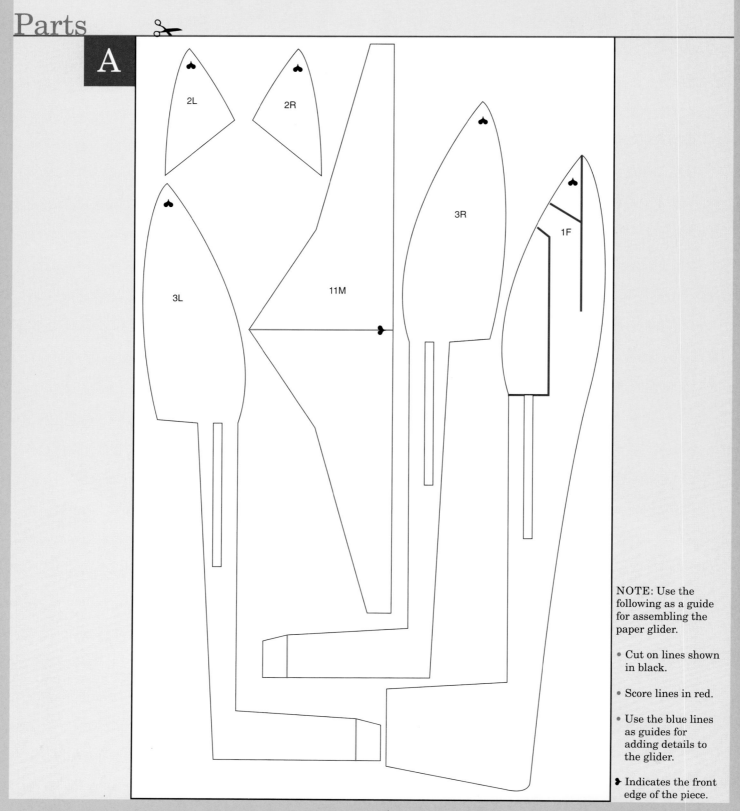

NOTE: Use the following as a guide for assembling the paper glider.

- Cut on lines shown in black.
- Score lines in red.
- Use the blue lines as guides for adding details to the glider.
- Indicates the front edge of the piece.

First, photocopy these two pages and the following page (100% size).

Then cut out the portion indicated below from the photocopy.
This makes a cutting guide for the various parts and fits a
standard 5 x 8 inch index card. See page 89 for step two.

Parts

B

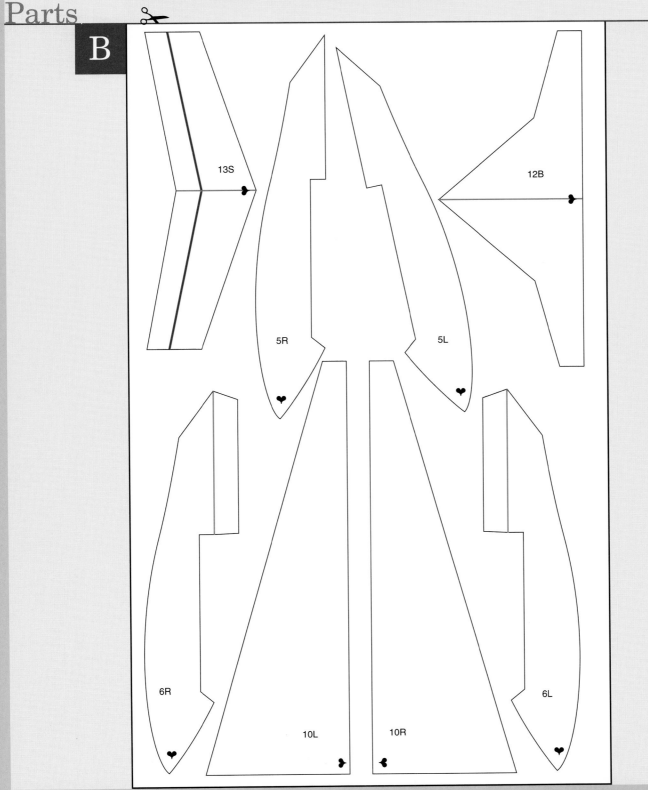

Schemp-Hirth Nimbus 4

Parts

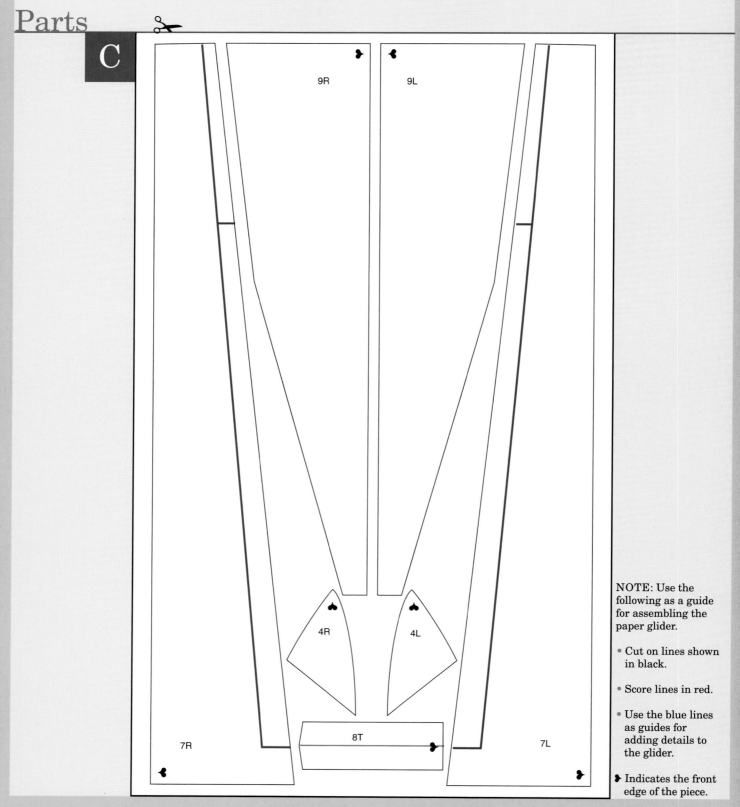

C

9R

9L

4R

4L

8T

7R

7L

NOTE: Use the following as a guide for assembling the paper glider.

- Cut on lines shown in black.

- Score lines in red.

- Use the blue lines as guides for adding details to the glider.

➤ Indicates the front edge of the piece.

HANDLING PAPER GLIDERS

Pick up and hold paper gliders by the nose, their sturdiest part. *Never* lift them by the wings or tail; this will distort their aerodynamic shape.

PREFLIGHT INSPECTION

After a paper glider is finished and the glue completely dried, do a preflight inspection and make any necessary adjustments.

Examine the glider thoroughly from the front, back, top, bottom, and each side. Check for parts that appear bent or twisted. Correct any defects. Gently massage the paper to work out bends and twists. Each side must be *exactly* like the other — shape, size, camber, dihedral — a paper glider must be symmetrical.

TEST FLIGHTS

The objective of test flights is to trim (adjust) the glider for straight and level flight at *its best speed* .

Hold the fuselage between thumb and forefinger just behind the plane's center of gravity. Throw it *gently* with a straight ahead motion (not as though it were a baseball). A glider flies best at only one speed. Throwing it too hard will cause it to climb sharply, stall, and dive to the ground, or do a complete loop. Once you have trimmed the glider for good flight performance, different throwing techniques can be tried. Try to test fly in calm conditions so that each flight is more predictable.

Sometimes, on the very first flight, a paper plane is unbalanced in every way at the same time. Therefore it is necessary to separate the control functions in one's mind and deal with them one at a time. (See page 22.)

To correct a dive, in a regular glider, the elevator needs adjusting by bending it up slightly to give positive trim (most of the paper gliders in this book) and down slightly for positive trim in a canard (the Solitaire). Continue making test flights concentrating on this one adjustment until this control input is correct. In normal gliding flight there should be slight positive elevator trim.

If a paper glider banks and turns in either direction it is always due to one wing producing more lift than the other. First make sure that the camber is *identical* in both wings along their entire lengths. If camber is slightly greater in one wing, that wing will produce more lift, causing it to rise — the plane will bank and turn in the opposite direction. Second, make sure that the wings are not twisted. The wingtip that is lower at the trailing edge (thereby having a greater angle of attack) will cause that wing to produce more lift, and it will rise — the plane will bank and turn in the opposite direction. Untwist the wings to correct this problem. Continue making test flights concentrating on this adjustment until the wings are correct.

A slightly bent fuselage will also cause the plane to turn by yawing left or right. Make the fuselage as straight as possible. For a final correction adjust the rudder by bending it in the opposite direction to the turn.

The paper gliders in this book are designed to last a long time. To keep them from becoming damaged when not in use they need proper storage. One way is to hang them by the nose from a line using clothes pins.

POWER LAUNCHING

Just as full-sized gliders were catapulted into the air using shock cords as a source of power in the days before aerotowing, paper gliders can be launched using a catapult made with an elastic band. This is an alternative to the hand-thrown high launch. Using this method, the direction of the launch 45 degrees upward and across the wind is similar to the hand launch method.

First prepare the glider by adding a tow hook. The glue used to build the glider must be *completely* dry for this (at least one day). Use an ordinary map pin (short head pin). Insert it into the nose of the glider in the approximate location shown in figure 15. Additional glue may be needed to keep it in place. To make the catapult, tie an elastic band to a stick such as a wooden dowel. See figure 16.

To launch, hold the glider between thumb and forefinger by the fuselage from underneath at the tail end. Hold the catapult stick in the other hand, loop the elastic over the head of the pin, stretch the band, and release the glider. Care must be taken not to over-speed the glider. If it flutters, use less tension.

Figure 15
Adding a tow hook

Insert a map pin into the heavy part of a glider's nose, in the direction indicated and as far forward as is practical for each glider type, leaving just the head sticking out. This is the tow hook.

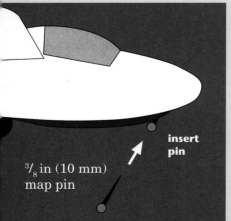

$^3/_8$ in (10 mm) map pin

insert pin

If the glider climbs, loses speed, and pitches down sharply (stalls), the elevator needs to be bent down slightly. However, if this problem cannot be corrected without the elevator being bent down below the straight level, the airplane's center of gravity is too far back and additional ballast is needed in the nose. Glue additional layers of paper into the nose. Again, continue making test flights until this problem is corrected.

Continue to make test flights until the plane flies straight and level in a gentle glide.

EXTENDING THE GLIDE

Full-sized gliders are always launched into the wind. If a paper glider is launched into the wind the increased relative airspeed would make the lightweight paper glider climb very steeply, and perhaps stall, and dive to the ground, or, if the elevator is bent up slightly, do a complete loop. When launched with the wind, wind speed is added to actual airspeed, increasing the ability to cover distance over the ground. But in a downwind launch the glider may stall if the wind is too strong because of the decreased relative airspeed. To avoid these tendencies, launch the glider across the wind, letting it turn downwind gradually.

Another way to fly a paper glider is to begin the flight with a high launch. The glider should be trimmed for a gentle left or right turn. (If the pilot is right-handed, trim for a gentle turn to the left.) For making a left turn adjust the control surfaces. (See page 22.)

Make these trim adjustments in very slight increments until the desired turn rate is achieved.

Launch the glider in an inclined position with considerable force upward and away from your body (about 45 degrees), across the wind. It gains altitude from the force of the throw, but loses speed as it climbs. The dihedral causes the wings to level out. Once level, the left-handed trim banks the glider into a gentle turn downwind at the top of its climb. Because of the altitude gained by the high launch, the descent should be a good long glide.

With a high launch it is also possible for a paper glider to become a sailplane and soar.

When the sun is shining, thermals can form almost anywhere, especially over dark colored fields, usually between 10 am and 4 pm (see page 36). If, after reaching the top of a launch, the glider spirals inside a bubble of rising air, it will climb even higher and extend its glide if the bubble is rising faster than the glider is descending. Some thermals are stronger than others and rise faster. The paper glider with the best glide ratio will be able to take advantage of the weakest thermals.

Because paper is a relatively unstable material it may be necessary to readjust the planes after every few flights. Gusty wind conditions can occur around strong thermals making it impossible to fly successfully such lightweight planes.

Aeronautical terms

Aerotow Towing a glider behind a powered airplane used as a method of launching the glider.

Aspect ratio The length of a wing in relation to its width. A square has an aspect ratio of 1:1.

Ailerons Surfaces on the trailing edges of the wings that control roll.

Airfoil A wing having a curved upper surface and usually a flat lower surface.

Angle of attack The downward slant, from front to back, of an airfoil to increase lift.

Angle of bank The raising of the outside wing and the lowering of the inside wing during a turn.

Attitude The roll, pitch, and yaw of an aircraft in flight, and the direction it is pointing in relation to the horizon.

Ballast Extra weight in the nose of an aircraft used to adjust the center of gravity.

Bernoulli's Principle The decrease of a fluid's pressure as its rate of flow increases.

Canard An aircraft having a small set of wings ahead of the main wings.

Camber The curved upper surface of a wing.

Center of gravity The point on the aircraft where its weight appears to be concentrated.

Center of lift The point on the aircraft where its lift appears to be concentrated.

Chord The distance from front to back of a wing.

Control surfaces Small flat hinged surfaces on the wings and tail used to maintain equilibrium and maneuver an aircraft.

Dihedral angle The upward slanting of wings away from the fuselage.

Drag The resistance of air on moving objects.

Elevator Control surface on the trailing edge of the horizontal stabilizer used to adjust pitch.

Fuselage The body of an airplane.

Gravity The force of the earth keeping objects on the ground and giving them weight.

Horizontal stabilizer A flat horizontal surface that directs the flow of air in aid of maintaining equilibrium.

Leading edge The front edge of a wing.

Lift The force generated by the wings that counteracts the force of gravity. Also, rising air currents used for soaring.

Maneuver Skilfully making an airplane move in the correct manner and fly in the desired direction.

Pitch The rotation of an airplane causing its nose to go up or down.

Ridge lift Rising air currents over sloping ground used by gliders to remain airborne.

Roll The rotation of an airplane causing the wingtips to rise or fall.

Rudder Control surface on the trailing edge of the vertical stabilizer used to control yaw.

Shock cord An elastic rope used to launch gliders.

Spar The main frame that supports a wing.

Stall The condition that occurs when the angle of attack is too great.

Streamlining Making an airplane's shape smooth so that air can flow across it creating the least amount of drag possible.

Thermal lift Rising air currents over heated ground used by gliders to remain airborne.

Thrust The force needed to move an airplane forward.

Trailing edge The back edge of a wing.

Trim The adjustment of control surfaces so that an airplane in flight does not roll, pitch, or yaw.

Trim drag The drag created by the control surfaces.

Vertical stabilizer A flat vertical surface that directs the flow of air in aid of maintaining equilibrium.

Vortex Air that slips off the wingtips from the high pressure area below to the low pressure area above the wings, and swirls in a circular manner behind each wingtip.

Wave lift Rising air currents over mountains used by gliders to remain airborne.

Wing loading The amount of weight a given area of wing is required to lift.

Wing span The distance from wingtip to wingtip.

Yaw The rotation of an airplane causing its nose to go left or right.

Figure 16

Elastic band catapult launcher

Tie a long thin elastic band to one end of a short stick such as a wooden dowel. To keep the knot from coming undone, tape it in place.

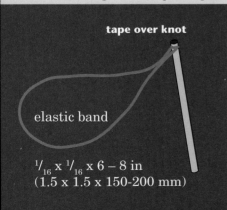

tape over knot

elastic band

$\frac{1}{16}$ x $\frac{1}{16}$ x 6 – 8 in
(1.5 x 1.5 x 150-200 mm)

Further Reading

BOOKS

Mackie, Dan. *Flight: Discover Planes, Hang Gliders, and Ultralights* Hayes, Burlington, 1986.

Schweizer, Paul A. *Wings Like Eagles*. Smithsonian, Washington, 1988.

Schmidt, Norman. *Discover Aerodynamics With Paper Airplanes*. Peguis, Winnipeg, 1991.

Schmidt, Norman. *Best Ever Paper Airplanes*. Sterling/Tamos, New York, 1994.

Schmidt, Norman. *Super Paper Airplanes*. Sterling/Tamos, New York, 1996.

Taylor, Michael. *History of Flight*. Crescent, New York, 1990.

PERIODICALS

Free Flight. The Soaring Association of Canada. Ottawa, bi-monthly.

Model Aviation. Academy of Model Aeronautics. Reston, monthly.

Sailplane & Gliding British Gliding Association. Leicester, bi-monthly.

Soaring. The Soaring Society of America. Hobbs, monthly.